-MAKING-
BIBLICAL
DECISIONS

Franklin E. Payne, Jr., M.D.

HOSANNAHOUSE

Making Biblical Decisions

Library of Congress Catalog Card Number: 89-84382
ISBN   0-9623204-0-4

Printed and bound in the United States of America

TABLE OF CONTENTS

To Hilton:

Champion of the truth, counselor,
physician, valued editor, and a dear friend.
With great gratitude.

Proverbs 27:6

CHAPTER 1

POPULATION CONTROL AND
THE CREATION MANDATE

In her wildest imagination Fanisi Kalusa could never have considered that she would become known world-wide.[1] In fact, her life centered around her tiny little village of Margoli, eight miles above the equator in western Kenya. She did, however, become known for her desire to have *20 children*, as she became the central subject of a documentary on world population (The money for which had been provided by the United Nations, the World Bank, and private donors.) Fanisi's village was located in "the middle of the most crowded farmland of the fastest growing nation in the history of the world." Her situation seemed perfect to portray what Robert McNamara described as the "rampant population growth (that left humanity) more certainly threatened than it has been by any catastrophe the world has yet endured."

> The question arises whether children should always be reared or may sometimes be exposed to die . . . . there should also be a law, in all states where the system of social habits is opposed to unrestricted increase, to prevent the exposure of children merely in order to keep the population down. The proper thing to do is to limit the size of each family.[2]

These words of Aristotle show that concern about population growth is not new. Perhaps it received its greatest momentum from Thomas Malthus' (1766-1834) "objective" studies and predictions about the sufficiencies of the earth to sustain the physical needs of his projected numbers. His conclusions and those of modern population planners, however, depend upon many assumptions and distortions. To complicate matters, eugenics has become linked with concern about population growth. Additional impetus came from increasing materialism that focuses on the "good life" when children absorb large sums that could be used for personal pleasure. Unfortunately, many Christians adopt these secular attitudes. We must, therefore, see what the Bible says about these matters.

You might ask, "How is population control related to medical ethics; isn't it properly a topic for social ethics?" Medicine is the means (birth control measures) to the end (population control). This chapter and the next form a unit, in which I shall analyze the ethics of population control as a goal and birth control methods as medical practice.

Fallacies of the Population Doomsdayers

First, predictions of future population numbers are extremely inaccurate. Malthus' initial projections, maintaining that the population of the earth would double every twenty-five years, have proved false.[3] If his predictions had been correct, the world's population would be sixty billion, nearly ten times what it actually is! Since 1973, the world's growth rate has slowed to 1.7 per cent (two per cent prior to that time) as fertility rates have dropped sharply in Asia and Latin America.[4] Contrary to views of United Nations planners, Colin Norman, a population expert, doubts that the world's population will ever double again.[5] Grounds for his position include increased death rates from war, famine, poor farming and fishing practices, as well as increased use of birth control measures (including abortion).

Second, the potential food supply of the world is far greater than previously realized. Colin Clark estimates that the world could sustain 35 billion people on the "overconsumptive" American diet and 100 billion on an "adequate" Japanese diet.[6] Malcolm Muggeridge considers Clark's arguments and data "unanswerable" and observes that they have never been seriously challenged.[7]

Third, the most serious hindrances to maximum food production are individual actions and national culture, particularly as determined by religion. Historically, famines are caused by war, the prevention of cultivation, the willful destruction of crops, defective agriculture, governmental interference by regulation or taxation, and currency restrictions.[8] Natural causes are the exception rather than the rule.

Consider the recent famine in Ethiopia. Traditionally, Ethiopian farmers stored food for the future years of crop failure that they knew were inevitable.[9] Under the present government, however, those who continued to store food were accused of "hoarding" and executed. Others trying to transport food were accused of "exploitation" and their goods confiscated. Sometimes, they were imprisoned or executed. Many young, able-bodied men were forced to leave their farms. Entrepreneurial incentives were dashed by widespread looting, confiscation, and expropriation. Both individual and business bank accounts were raided. Farmers were forced into collectives and associations. No plans for replacing the former storage of food or transportation to move food to needy areas were made. Even the massive gifts of food from other countries did not reach the people. It rotted on docks, was diverted to those in power, or was used to manipulate the populace.

Situations elsewhere also show that the major problem is individual, social, political, and religious. Dr. J. S. Kanwar of the Indian Agrarian Research Institute, concluded that modern methods of agriculture in two of the Federal States in India could produce enough food for the entire country. If the entire country used such methods, one-third of the crop would exceed the country's need and could be exported. Throughout the world the typical work day varies from 45 minutes to seven hours.[10] Obviously, longer working hours would produce a great deal more. Overfishing, overgrazing, deforestation and overploughing reduces productivity by destroying basic resources.[11]   Further, lack of productivity in the tropics has been attributed to the people who live there and is not due to the heat and humidity *per se*.[12]

Fourth, productivity is not necessarily limited where people are closely populated.

> There is an interesting theory according to which, from an economic point of view, countries can, on a certain level, be "overpopulated," then, within the framework of a more developed economy, become underpopulated, and with additional industrialization again become overpopulated, and so forth.[13]

This phenomenon may account for the fact that in the West "the birth-rate began to decrease a generation or so after the death-rate decreased without any help from contraceptives, abortion or other forms of birth-control."[14] (It is doubtful that abortion is effective as a birth control measure.[15])

The Netherlands and Japan, two of the most densely populated countries in the world, import workers to meet their productive capacity.[16] Tyrol, a federal state of Austria, was Central Europe's "poor-house," which in 1898 was unable to employ and feed its population.[17] Emigration was high. Today, lifestyle in a Tyrolean village is similar to life in the United States, a most remarkable reversal! Taiwan, two-thirds the size of Switzerland but with sixteen million people, has the second highest standard of living in Asia (behind Japan, another densely populated country).

Fifth, cultural upheavals have been caused by population planning because its acceptance and practice is uneven. Europeans, North Americans, Australians, Japanese, and South Africans have been practicing birth control, but few other countries do so to the same extent. The net result is that the "white races" and the Japanese face a declining percentage of the world's population.[18] "Genocide is now the fashion... (of these regions) in an undeclared warfare vis-a-vis an unborn generation."[19] In the Netherlands, Catholics "overtook" Protestants as the 20th century began because the latter used contraception and the former did not.

It would take us far afield and require a lengthy treatise to discuss the morality of these demographic changes. It is sufficient here to note that major shifts take place when population controls are attempted.

Sixth, food production has increased more rapidly than the population on a world-wide basis.[20] This fact substantiates the above observation that the major problem lies with people and their culture, not food production *per se.*

> It appears never to have occurred to them (the advocates of controlled population development) that the logical way out of the chronic situation in which there are more hungry people than food is not by way of reducing the population, but rather of increasing the production of the means of subsistence.[21]

Even in the United States where large surpluses of food are produced almost every year, more could be produced were it not for government controls. Often, the problem of insufficient food lies in a failure to deliver it to the people (see Ethiopia above). Transportation problems have to be addressed, as well.

Seventh, how can any "optimum" number for the population of a country or the world be determined? What objective standards could be used? How much land space, food, and other material goods should each person have? The ultimate question is *who will make these decisions?* The answer of the population planners is an elite group, usually composed of scientists, using expertise from the "objective" (meaning amoral) world of science to answer these far-reaching moral questions. It it fascinating, though dangerous, that strong advocates of pluralism are quite unwilling to employ a pluralistic approach in answering these questions. Such unwillingness clearly shows their adherance to an authoritarian philosophy that includes coercive tyranny to achieve their ends. (So much for pluralism!)

Eighth, it is not universally true that large families are "unwanted." Many people wish to have large families. This fact has caused a prominent feminist, Germaine Greer, to "change her tune." From a tour of rural villages in India

> she was deeply moved by a culture in which there were no "unwanted children," in which family life was strong and sex regarded as something other than an "indoor sport," in which the women's role in family and village life was important and honorable.[22]

Ninth, elderly rich and poor alike need their children to provide for them and to continue the economic development of their country.[23] Allan Carlson has calculated that the loss of 17 million children in the United States through abortion (who might have become producing adults) to be $1.45 trillion in national income, of which $291 billion would have been federal income tax. Consider this amount relative to the current budget deficit of $150-$200 billion dollars a year.[24] He has called this loss, "The Malthusian Deficit." His calculations include many assumptions, but the value of his work is to give some objectivity to the enormous potential "wealth" to our country from larger families.

Julian Simon has briefly summarized other arguments.[25] His answers to the question, "Why is population rhetoric so appealing?" includes: short-run vs. long-run costs, apparent consensus of expert judgment, population as a cause of pollution, judgments about people's rationality, media exposure, money, and standards of proof and rhetoric. To the question, "What are the underlying reasons for doomsday fears and rhetoric?," he answers: simple world-saving humanitarianism, taxation fears, supposed economic and political self-interest, fear of communism, dislike of business, belief in the superiority of "natural processes," religious antagonisms, racism, the belief of the more educated that they know what is best for the less educated, lack of historical perspective, and fitness of the human race.

In conclusion, numbers per se are not the disease, so birth control (especially abortion) is not the cure. The fact is, the cure is worse than the problem. There are hidden agendas, motives, and severe distortions of facts. Allan Carlson calls us to action.

> Christians . . . face a special imperative in ending the Malthusian charade. Its core assumption – that man alone is vile and nature alone is holy – represents a corruption of Christian truth.[26]

The Creation Mandate

"And God blessed them; and God said to them, "Be fruitful and multiply, and fill the earth . . ." (Gen. 1:28a). This directive is one of seven given to Adam and Eve prior to their Fall: the replenishing of the earth (Gen. 1:28a), subduing of the same (Gen. 1:28a), dominion over the creatures (Gen. 1:28b), labor (Gen. 2:15), the weekly Sabbath (Gen. 2:3), and marriage (Gen. 2:24-25). They are called "creation mandates" by some theologians and "orders of creation" by others. Our focus is on the command to procreate. It is inseparable from the seventh.[27] When God limited one man to one woman and vice-versa, He limited procreation to this union. In the next section we will explore the relationship of that union to the family.

Since these mandates are not taught widely today, they may be unfamiliar to you. Likely, however, you will recognize principles that Scripture presents elsewhere. You may recognize general principles of "Christian" responsibility that had not yet been crystallized in your mind. Too many Christians have been

"brain-washed" by the population myths and birth control advocates. The creation mandate is the basic biblical principle by
which to replace these distortions.

Some may wonder whether these mandates continue intact
after the Fall wreaked havoc with the whole cosmos – (Rom.
8:20), including its perfect moral structure. Some modification
seems necessary from Jesus' allowance for divorce (Mt. 19:1-12).
First, He states the creation mandate for marriage (v. 4-6). Then,
He upholds the allowance for divorce under Mosaic law, " . . .
because of your hardness of heart" (v. 8). Again, He states the
creation mandate, "but from the beginning it has not been this
way" (v. 8). Finally, he re-states the Old Testament sanction for
divorce when adultery has occurred. Man's sin has made divorce
a practical necessity in some cases of adultery. (Paul added
desertion of an unbeliever as a cause for divorce.[28]

Since Jesus modified one creation mandate because of man's
sinfulness, one might expect some modification of the command
to "be fruitful and multiply." Helmut Thielicke apparently takes
this position when he says that this command is "confronted with
concrete situations which resist its realization."[29] We should not,
however, rush to this conclusion. Concerning divorce, Jesus
Himself makes an *explicit* modification. *There is no such explicit
modification concerning "fruitfulness."* Christians do not have the
prerogative to modify God's commands without explicit biblical
instructions.

Further, we should not resort to the choice of "lesser evils,"[30]
where the situation seems to offer only choices that are each evil.
God never places us in such a position. Dr. John Jefferson Davis'
principle of "contextual absolutism" "holds that in each and every
ethical situation, no matter how extreme, there is a course of
action that is morally right and free of sin"[31] (I Cor. 10:31).
Finding that course may be extremely difficult, but Davis calls us
to the "cost of discipleship . . . in the twentieth century American

church, where believers are all too often tempted by the comforts and compromises of the surrounding culture."[32]

The creation mandate remains in effect.[33] Its repetition after the Fall and after the flood clearly underscores its continuance. It applies to both believers and unbelievers since it was given to the natural father (Adam) and mother (Eve) of the human race. Since unbelievers are not likely to respond to biblical authority, conscious fulfillment of this creation mandate falls to believers. There are many reasons why believers should be concerned about its fulfillment, some of which we will review after we develop a biblical concept of the family.

The Biblical Concept of The Family

We start with "the beginning." In Genesis 2 God clearly states the purpose of marriage, ". . . it is not good for the man to be alone; I will make him a helper suitable for him!" (v.18). Then, God made Eve to complement Adam in every way; "meet" means "appropriate to, corresponding to or approximating at every point."[34] That is, the man would be lonely and incomplete without his wife. She is his "companion" (Prov. 2:17) and he is her "companion" (Malachi 2:14). Further, that " . . . the two shall become one flesh" (Gen. 2:24) indicates the unity of this companionship. Since "flesh"[35] refers to individual persons (Gen. 6:17, 7:22, 8:21; Acts 2:17), to "become one flesh" means that the husband and wife become as one person: physically as they live together and enjoy a sexual relationship as they care for each others' hurts and needs, intellectually as they share and complement each other's life. John Calvin commenting upon Mt. 19:5-6 states, " . . . whoever divorces his wife (or husband) tears himself in pieces, because such is the force of holy marriage, that the husband and wife become one man."[36] The "two persons come to think, act, feel as one."[37] Thus, marriage is primarily a functional and physical companionship in all the endeavors of both "till death do you part." This "one flesh" unity is earthly unity, not eternal (Lk. 20:34-36).

The strength of this companionship is emphasized in its designation as a covenant (Malachi 2:14). God chose the covenant as the means by which He would establish His relationship with the nation of Israel (Gen. 17:1-14) and spiritual "Israel" (all believers, Gal. 3:29). Thus, marriage is a covenant that reflects God's plan of salvation. Even further, marriage reflects the relationship within the Trinity (I Cor. 11:3).

A secondary function of this unity is the propagation and rearing of children. The Roman Catholic Church and some Protestants wrongly teach that procreation is the primary purpose of marriage. First, children are a temporary part of marriage because they eventually leave home, whereas marriage continues for the lifetimes of the husband and wife. In fact, the children are instructed to "leave" (separate) from their parents and "cleave" (join) themselves to their spouses (Gen. 2:24). Second, marriage is not necessary, biologically, for the propagation of the human race. The prevalence of illegitimate births and the reproductive techniques clearly cover this reality.

The sexual relationship is also secondary. Obviously, marriage is not necessary for the act of intercourse, but God designed marriage for its fullest and only means of expression. Sexual fulfillment flows out of the companionship of the husband and the wife. In this context of fulfillment and commitment children are conceived. It is not, however, the only dimension of the physical relationship. Couples who are unable to have sexual intercourse can still have a deeply physical relationship through touches, embraces, and other physical contact. It is the erotic focus of our society that centers on marriage as a sexual relationship. The Bible does not place the emphasis on sex even though it is not embarrassed by the pleasures and ecstasies of sex, as vividly portrayed in the Song of Solomon.

Finally, marriage is the basic unit of society and the smallest unit of government. Education, discipline and justice, health, and economics are administered there. A man's ability to govern his family is a prerequisite for his governing the church (I Tim. 3:4-5) and by implication, any other social sphere.

In conclusion, marriage was instituted of God as a lifelong design, primarily for companionship and complementary work. It is a covenant of companionship. A man or woman is incomplete until he or she has married (unless gifted by God to serve Him without a spouse, Mt. 19:12, I Cor. 7:7). Children and sexual fulfillment are functions of this unity, but a marriage can be fully complete without either. The marriage and the family form the basic unit of society and government; any enhancement or disruption of the family multiplies far beyond itself for this reason. To be biblical, medical ethics must incorporate this companionship concept of the family.

Implications of the Creation Mandate and the Biblical Family

Bob's problem (he had come alone for counsel) was unusual: his wife did not want children at this time. He had been married to Jane for six years and until the last few months, both had agreed not to have children. He had been in school most of that time while she worked to support him. Now, they were both working, their debts were paid, and he wanted children. Jane, however, seemed to enjoy buying things for the house that she had always wanted and knew the expense of a baby would interfere with her plans. Bob was concerned that they might wait too long since Jane had two medical problems that could interfere with conception and decrease their chances of having any children at all. As I gathered more data, it was apparent that the presenting problem reflected other problems in the marriage.

This type of case was the first for me, but I made some usual suggestions to improve their communication, partly to buy time for me to talk over their situation with other elders. Bob and Jane were to come together to the next counseling session. As matters turned out, I never saw them again formally. Evidently, Bob's visit was stimulus enough for Jane to re-think her position. Within a few months she was obviously pregnant and they now have two children.

Jane is not alone in her views. What does the Creation Mandate have to say to them?

Involuntary Childlessness Because of Physical Inability. Because physical inability to have children does not detract from the primary purpose of marriage, the fullness of the husband-wife relationship is not necessarily diminished. Further, even though the couple is not able to obey the creation mandate, their situation does not involve sin because personal sin is never ascribed when failure to fulfill a biblical command is completely beyond physical capability.

Voluntary Childlessness. A different situation is the couple that (like Jane) voluntarily chooses not to have children. Such is a violation of the creation mandate. Thielicke claims that such a marriage should not take place.[38] A man and woman who contemplate marriage without the intention to have children, even though that may be rare, have insufficient biblical grounds for marriage. Although they could still fulfill the primary purpose of marriage, they would possibly be in continual violation of the biblical command to procreate.

Some qualifications, however, are in order. Thielicke mentioned several "exceptional" cases: severe illness of the mother, severe hereditary affliction, economic circumstances which will not permit the rearing of another child even with the greatest frugality, early marriages (that is, by students), housing difficulties, and job situations.[39] The most valid is the severe illness in the mother. In this situation, the choice is between the new life of a child and the life of the mother. The choice is similar to the one that is faced when a mother's life is threatened if her pregnancy is continued. Other limitations on this creation mandate also apply.

Genetic Inheritance. Arbitrarily, I will divide this limitation into three categories. Into the first falls the couple whose first child unexpectedly has a genetic disorder or congenital abnormality (a problem or set of problems that occurs during the development of the baby in the mother's womb or the birth process, and is not an inherited condition.) The difficulty that such a child places on the couple financially, physically, socially and spiritually may be sufficient to limit their having additional children. This limitation is strengthened if there is a high probability that they will have another child with a genetic disorder. If, however, it is virtually certain that additional children will be normal, they may want more.

The second category involves couples who have not yet had children, but know that they have a very high probability of having a child with a genetic disorder. This second category as a limitation is not as strong as the first because the above couple has already acted upon the creation mandate. Usually, the stress of genetically-abnormal children is outweighed by unexpected benefits, as with Down syndrome children. We do not want to say categorically, with Paul Ramsey, that this second couple should have a child.[40]

In a third category is an older couple with an increased risk of genetic aberrations because of age. These rates are commonly given according to the age of the mother, although the age of the man is a factor in genetic abnormalities, as well. When the woman is 35 years of age, the chances of a "clinically significant abnormality" is 0.5 percent (5/1000 births); at 40 years 1.5 percent (1.5/1000); at 45 years 5.0 percent (50/1000); and at 49 years 13.0 percent (77/1000).[41] For the couple without any children, these "odds" would not seem to warrant childlessness. These "odds" are considerably less than those inherited abnormalities that may affect

25-100 percent of all offspring. Of course, all other factors that we are discussing here would have to be considered. Having children at older ages should certainly not be undertaken lightly.

There are too many variables to cover every situation. Most genetic abnormalities are not severe. In fact everyone has several hidden genetic defects. It would seem that the expected disorder would have to be severe (multiple organ systems affected) to prevent the couple from having children. The couple would have to consider their own physical, financial, and spiritual resources. They should talk with other Christians who have these children. Most importantly, they should seek counsel from their local church officers who are their God-ordained spiritual advisors.

Postponed Child-Bearing. Certain situations may require postponed childlessness. 1) A year is needed to allow for a new husband and wife to learn to live together (Dt. 24:5). Although this passage has to do with military and civil duties, it probably represents a general principle that allows a new husband and wife to enjoy and get to know each other without excessive demands that interfere with their relationship.

2) Immediately successive pregnancies may be difficult for some women both physically and spiritually. It would seem appropriate to plan some spacing between children. But this decision seems to be one that each couple is entirely free to make as they consider their abilities and resources.

3) The loss of a job, or other financial loss, may temporarily reduce a family's means to have another child. Again, this decision is one that couples are free to make. Many relevant factors vary considerably from family to family, so their choices here will also vary.

4) A modern limitation is the time needed to complete lengthy educational requirements, especially those that require several years in addition to the usual four years of college. This situation usually requires one spouse to work, thus effectively straining the financial or spiritual resources for raising children. Surely, because

of the command in I Cor. 7:9b the better choice is to marry and postpone children than to be sexually frustrated. Couples should be careful, however, that careers do not indefinitely extend this situation. They should also be aware that ten percent of married couples have physical difficulties that may inhibit conception. To wait may decrease their chances to have any children at all.

How Many Children? How many children should a couple have? Likely, two are insufficient unless there are biblically-legitimate limiting factors. The word, "multiply" (Hebrew, *rabah*), used in the creation mandate, means "to multiply, become numerous, become great . . . . Basically, this word connotes numerical increase."[42] I am tempted to say that "multiply" means a greater increase than simple "addition." The impression is one of large numbers. Even so, large numbers of people may be achieved by increasing life expectancy or by large numbers of children. So practically, "multiply" does not help to determine the number of children that a couple should have. It does, however, seem to imply several.

Psalm 127 implies the same. A "warrior" is not likely to have only one or two arrows and say that his "quiver is full" (v. 5). Further, he would probably not go into battle or go hunting with only one or two. Another element in the psalm is the blessedness that many children bring. Certainly, this description of children is far removed from that of many population planners who speak of them as "burdens."

Two conclusions seem warranted. First, Psalm 127 emphasizes the expectation and blessedness of many children. Second, population analysts have concluded that two children will not result in numerical growth. Putting these two conclusions together (with far more emphasis on the first than the second), we would say that at least three children are expected of God's people *who otherwise do not face the concrete limitations that we have outlined.* What is necessary is that this psalm be taken seriously by each couple as they prayerfully decide what number God would expect them to have. In addition, other substantive reasons call for large families.

1) Every society needs the moral influence of children raised in the "discipline and instruction of the Lord" (Eph. 6:4). Of course, Christian children are not always so raised, but recent interest in biblical principles for the home and Christian education gives us hope for improvement. Today's emphasis on birth and population control is a great opportunity for the advancement of Christianity. With larger, properly-trained families Christians can become a larger percentage of society, advancing the Christian worldview that has given rise to the greatness of the Western world. At a lesser level, large families are necessary for Christians to defend themselves against staunch, widespread opposition to the Bible as a basis of morality and law.[43]

2) God's primary fulfillment of the Great Commission (Mt. 28:18-20) is through the family.

> The marital institution is sanctified by the forces of redemptive grace to such an extent that it is made one of the main channels for the accomplishment of God's saving purpose in the world.[44]

The application of the following Proverb seems appropriate to this purpose:

> In a multitude of people is a king's glory
> But in a dearth of people is a prince's ruin (Prov. 14:28).

Christians who are unfamiliar with Covenant Theology may not know that God's promises in the Old Testament were covenantal. That is, He made covenants with certain people *and* their "seed" (Gen. 9:9, 17:7, 35:12). The inclusion of children is also clear in the New Testament (Acts 2:39). Certainly, the discipleship inherent in the Great Commission is potentially the most thorough for the children of Christians.

3) Parents can be more easily cared for by several children if they become unable to provide for themselves. This biblical picture seems foreign because our culture has distorted the continuing relationship of the extended family, and placed the responsibility on the federal government (e.g. Social Security). Nevertheless, Christians are not allowed to shirk their God-given responsibilities (I Tim. 5:8).

4) There are advantages for the children too. Of necessity, children learn to share, since in large families they have fewer "things." They must interact more frequently and with more personalities in close situations. They must earn more spending money for themselves. With this training, after they leave home they will have more potential resources for help should difficult circumstances arise. Since children have sinful natures, more problems will occur with more children, yet the advantages outweigh the disadvantages.

Myths against large families. Arguments against large families are made by our non-Christian culture. First, we are told there are already (or soon will be) too many people on the earth. This argument has been dealt with already. Second, raising children is prohibitively expensive today.[45] There is some truth to this argument, but it assumes a great deal. Basic necessities are food, clothing, shelter, and education. Expenses, however, do not increase proportionally to numbers. Clothes can be handed down. Two or more children can share the same room. Food is proportionally less expensive when bought in larger quantities and the more expensive foods are not necessary for balanced nutrition. College education may be desirable, but many trades and other jobs do not require a college education. Children may also earn a large portion of (if not all) these costs themselves. Certainly, some lifestyles would be radically altered, but what is our standard: our culture or God's Word? If children are a gift and blessing from the Sovereign Lord, does it not stand to reason that He will provide for them?

Many Chinese families demonstrate that large families can meet these challenges. Brought to this country as manual laborers, they became entrepreneurs, developing small, successful businesses *primarily within family units* and have provided their children with excellent educations, including college and graduate school. They are able to distinguish between "wants" and "needs," a trait almost foreign to our materialistic culture.

The local church is an untapped resource. The biblical order of responsibility is first for one's family (I Tim. 5:8), then for other believers (Gal. 6:10), and then for the remainder of society. The family is not an isolated unit but part of the local church, primarily, and the universal church, secondarily. Certainly, a mature local church is rare.[46] The removal of our materialistic orientation and the development of vital local churches would provide necessary resources for greater numbers of children in Christian families.

Third, we are fooling ourselves with the notion of "control" and "planning."

> . . . the attempt to control our reproductive capabilities *without* controlling ourselves is based on self-deception. For there are all sorts of possibilities beyond our capacity to predict, let alone regulate. The financial drain anticipated from the birth of a child may be bypassed or surmounted by an unexpected promotion, a change in jobs, or a son's decision to become a policeman instead of a Ph.D. Or the undreamed of, unexpected rewards of child-rearing may more than reconcile the parent to a flatter billfold. Or it may be as bad or worse than anticipated. But how does one know beforehand? How does one ever know?[47]

Has our technological age blinded us to the reality of God's ultimate and final Sovereignty? He "works all things after the counsel of His will" (Eph. 1:11) and controls the affairs of nations (Ps. 2:1-12). As Christians, He "causes all things [even our sins and failures] to work together for [our] good" (Rom. 8:28). Certainly, planning is proper Christian stewardship, but we have seen that in the use of birth control we have tended to forget God's commands and His ultimate control. Even so, whether from teaching or the Sovereign movement of God's Spirit, it is my observation that Christians are having many more than the "allotted" 1-2 children.

Summary. It would be impossible to deal particularly with all the relevant decisions that couples face. I can, however, develop some general principles for use in particular instances. First, any couple who marries and chooses not to have children, even though they are physically able or do not have a severely limiting situation, violates God's creation mandate. On the one hand, contraception is never forbidden in the Bible. On the other hand, the emphasis of the Bible is on the blessing of many children. Second, one or two children are probably insufficient to fulfill the biblical expectation. "The burden of proof rests, then, on the couple who wish to restrict the size of their family."[48] Third, any limitation of children should not be made without counsel from one's local church. The final decision rests on the family, however, not on the church.[49] The church should advise, not dictate. Fourth, the responsibility to procreate was given to the *family.* The state has no authority to set *any limits whatsoever* on the *size of families.*[50]

Conclusions: Biblical Perspectives

The creation mandate is consistent with the principles and facts even of those who oppose population control. Although clear biblical teaching does not need outside support, such consistency gives additional assurance that our interpretation is correct. Science and Scripture ultimately cannot conflict.[51] Such consistency also provides non-biblical answers for opponents who do not believe that the Bible has valid arguments.

The creation mandate must be accepted by faith. In spite of evidence that the world can support 35-100 billion people, the hypothesis remains untested. We would be dishonest if we did not consider that the population controllers *might* be right. In the end, assurance does not come from our "planning" and calculation, but from the trustworthiness of God.

Such trust has two applications. First, His laws and general principles cannot be compromised because of personal or social situations. For example, induced abortion can never be justified for any reason because it violates the Sixth Commandment.[52] Individual families, however, may have limiting factors. Second, at the appropriate time God will enable faithfulness for the fulfillment of His commandments. One conclusion of our study is that population growth is quite unpredictable. Further, food production can be markedly increased by current methods, and future technology is likely to cause further increase.

We frequently overlook the fact that we live in a universe where the primary reality is supernatural. The Trinity and created spiritual beings existed prior to this universe and will continue to do so after it is gone or changed by fire. Certain conditions are predicated on God's supernaturalism. One example is the Sabbath. As Christians, we almost entirely associate the Sabbath with Sunday, our day of worship and rest, but the concept of the Sabbath also concerned rest for the fields (Lev. 25:1-22). American farmers confirm that land will produce a greater harvest in the year that follows its lying fallow. There is no naturalistic explanation for this phenomenon.[53]

On this basis of natural effect by supernatural cause, is it not logical to assume that God *will provide for the fulfillment of the creation mandate*? This, of course, is a matter of faith, but not too much for one who has "evidence of things not seen" (Heb. 11:1). It is not a blind leap, but a conclusion based upon the character of God and His activity in the affairs of men and nature as revealed in the Bible.

The "bottom line" for sinful men is that they believe they are able to plan the growth of the world's population better than God. This deception is one aspect of God's supposed "foolishness" and man's supposed "wisdom" (I Cor. 1:25-31). Placed in this perspective, it is truly foolish to follow man's wisdom.

The perspective grows clearer when the population and birth control planners are placed within their own worldview. Ultimately, they are the advocates of state coercion and death (by abortion, infanticide, and euthanasia) as a solution to social problems. Their practical solutions represent a philosophical (actually, religious) system that is opposed to the biblical worldview. There are only two such systems.[54] As Harry Blamires has said, there is a "gigantic battle between good and evil that splits the universe."[55] The population debate is one "front" of that battle.

God holds the family responsible for fulfilling the creation mandate. This fact alone is sufficient to counter any government mandate or even encouragement of birth control by its citizens. It is a family responsibility that the state must not assume. Later, we will see how this principle applies to carriers of genetic diseases and those who are mentally incompetent.

For population planners to advocate state control is consistent with their anti-life, anti-family worldview (revealed in their advocacy of heterosexual activity outside marriage). It is no accident that legally minor children are not required to obtain their parental permission to receive birth control prescriptions, to be treated for sexually transmitted diseases, or to have an abortion. Only where the family and its procreative task is denigrated could this be possible. Once again, we see the imposition of man's design over God's.

Evangelicals must recognize population explosion as an evangelistic opportunity. Today, there are more means than ever to proclaim the Good News worldwide. Directly, we have seen that

God's primary means of evangelism is the family. Indirectly, evangelism takes place outside the family. An increasing number of people may mean a potential increase in the number of people who may be brought into God's Kingdom.

"Wrongful Birth"

The euphemism, "wrongful birth,"[56] illustrates anti-life and anti-family sentiment. The attitude has shifted from children as blessings to children as wrongs to the degree that tort damages are sought for both healthy and "defective" children.[57] In fact, courts have ruled that wrongful birth can result for eight different reasons: failure to fill a birth control prescription, an unsuccessful sterilization, an unsuccessful vasectomy, inaccurate pre-pregnancy counseling, inaccurate pregnancy counseling, failure to diagnose a pregnancy, failure to offer amniocentesis to a woman whose age makes her a "high-risk" pregnancy, and . . . unsuccessful abortion. Mostly, this change has taken place within the last twenty years.

Contrast these successful court cases with the following case in 1934. A man underwent a vasectomy to prevent the conception of another child after his wife had "substantial difficulty" with her first pregnancy. When his wife later conceived and had a normal, healthy child, he sued for damages from the physician who had done the vasectomy. He lost the case because a vasectomy was against public policy (how times have changed!). As recently as 1967, a couple sued their doctors on the grounds that they were negligent to inform them of the possible harmful effects of German measles on an unborn child so that they could have had an abortion. This couple lost because

> the intangible, unmeasureable, and complex human benefits of motherhood and fatherhood . . . (weigh) against the alleged emotional and money injuries . . . . substantial public policy

reasons prevent this Court from allowing damages for the denial of the opportunity to take an embryonic life [to have an abortion].

Today, the mother has the legal right to "take an embryonic life!"

If the concept of wrongful life continues, it will take its toll on human values. 1) Increasing pressure will be exerted on women over 35, whose babies have a increased likelihood of genetic problems, to have amniocentesis for all pregnancies to evaluate the quality of the fetus with a view to aborting those with genetic "defects." 2) Infanticide will become the "solution" for those who are born in spite of attempts to detect and to prevent their births. 3) The effect may be severe on the child who becomes aware that his birth was "wrong." 4) Benefits for handicapped people may deteriorate. 5) Physicians could lose their legal right not to participate in or perform abortions.

6) The astronomical awards of these suits are already raising the costs of malpractice insurance for obstetricians and gynecologists so high that some are leaving their practice. To continue to deliver babies, they must raise fees to cover this "overhead." The problem extends to midwives, so the availability of professionals to manage pregnancy and deliver babies may become inadequate. 7) A larger dimension of the same concept is that children have the "right" to sue their parents for wrongful birth. Although such action is just beginning in this country, it is already widespread in Sweden. The corresponding breakdown of the family in which a child can sue his parents for such reasons is barbaric.

The concept of a wrongful birth is foreign to God's creation mandate, His blessing through children, and His design for the family.

Sexual Research and Therapy

Lack of response to sexual research and therapy by Christians reveals the depth to which we have been influenced by modern society. Under the guise of "desensitization," video presentations are made at medical and other professional meetings that would be "XXX-rated" in a movie theater. The overflow crowds that attend these showings are evidence that interest is more than "academic."

The first such "research" to achieve scientific status was the Kinsey Report in 1953.[58] It is still quoted as a factual source, but few scrutinize it to determine how its "facts" were obtained. Dr. S. I. McMillen is one exception.[59] He outlines the extreme bias present in Kinsey's work: 1) the ratio of single women to married women was three times greater than the general population and 2) the only participants were those women who were willing to report the intimacies of their sexual experience. Yet, from this study norms were established for sexually "fulfilled" women.

Today, the most prominent sexual researchers are the husband and wife team of William H. Masters and Virginia Johnson. Their research is immoral since it includes the study of sexual partners who are not married. Even a husband and wife who are willing to be studied under the scrutiny of others violate the intimacy that God has directed for marriage (Heb. 13:4). A morality that allows unmarried partners to engage in sexual "research" is nothing less than perversion.

Before going further, you should understand that the Bible is not prudish about sex. The Song of Solomon is quite descriptive of intimacies between two lovers. A recent book has explored the various sexual themes of this book in some detail.[60] In this biblical light the Puritans have been wrongly maligned for their supposedly restrictive attitude toward sexual behavior. In fact, this inaccurate view ascribes to the Puritans attitudes that actually reflect the Victorian era. God does restrict sexual activity to marriage, but His design for the fullest and most joyous expression of sexual fulfillment is not restrictive!

Evidence for the association of a strong religious commitment and enjoyment of sexual intimacy comes from an unlikely source, *Redbook Magazine*.[61] In its first report *of all age groups*, "strongly religious women were the most likely to describe their marital sex as 'very good.'" In its second report, women were "asked about religious feelings in a more complex way," but the results confirmed the first report that no other group had better sexual relationships than those who were "strongly or moderately religious." On the opposite side "the women with strong feelings against religion were the likeliest to have unhappy sexual relationships."

Two characteristics of these studies should be noted. First, "religious" people in the United States are predominately Christians in spite of our increasingly religious pluralism. Second, *Redbook Magazine*, as it promotes the modern "sexual ethic," would not be likely to try to refute the long-held (but erroneous) view that strongly religious women are sexually "up-tight." Thus, *Redbook* as the source gives greater credence to the validity of the study and credits them with honest reporting.

Unfortunately, some evangelicals adopt views of sexual activity within marriage that reflect secular, rather than biblical thinking. Dr. Robert Smith's review of one such book illustrates this situation.[62] Although he makes a thorough review of the book to show many biblical and unbiblical principles, we will only examine two problems that are especially serious. First, the title of the book, *The Act of Marriage* reflects the perception that sexual fulfillment is the central focus of marriage. Dr. Smith correctly states that

> the act of marriage is the binding of two people together in a lifelong companionship, and as a result of that bond the sexual relationship will be a very vital part of their life.

Second, the authors use "lovemaking," "make love," and "loving" to identify sexual activities. This selection of terms is a serious limitation of the biblical concept of love. *Agape*, the predominant word in the New Testament for love, is used of the relationship of God to man (John 3:16), man to God (Mt. 22:37), man to man (Mt. 22:39), and spouse to spouse (Eph. 5:25). Certainly, within marriage one expression of agape is sexual, but the breadth and depth of the word is lost when it is limited to the sexual part of marriage. *Philos* is used much less often than agape, but is a synonym of agape if one considers that both are used similarly in various contexts.[63] The Greek word, *eros*, that is sometimes use to denote sexual love, is not present in the New Testament.

The virtual identification of "love" with sexual behavior is a secular concept, probably Freudian in origin, that should be avoided by Christians. Anyone experienced in marriage counseling knows that most sexual problems are secondary to other problems. This reality reflects the biblical concept that sexual behavior is an expression of marriage, not its central feature.

The biblical standard is absent from every area of medicine and sexual research/therapy. We do not question that sexual problems within Christian marriages need to be addressed and counseled, but biblical principles and definitions must control both analysis and direction. Current knowledge, gained from sexual research should not be ignored, but must be carefully scrutinized because of the immoral situations from which it was derived. At the same time further research in this area must be condemned. Sexual intimacy is reserved for marriage by the One who instituted marriage and to those believers whom He has given gifts to counsel such problems. It is a fallacy of modern thinking that we must have greater knowledge in every area than was available in the past in order to "cope." We have the same promise to us that

God gave to Paul, "My grace is sufficient for you, for power is perfected in weakness" (II Cor. 12:9a).

CHAPTER 2

BIRTH CONTROL: METHODS AND MORALITY

Bill and Sue were engaged to be married. In my pre-marital sessions with them I routinely covered various methods of birth control. Of course, the intra-uterine contraceptive device was not a serious consideration because it was clearly an abortifacient (see below). I had settled that issue in my own mind several years earlier. Now, however, Bill and Mary threw in a new wrinkle! They presented me with material (printed by a pro-life organization) that stated, without reservation, that birth control pills were abortifacients. This situation posed a real dilemma for me. Until this point I had had no moral problem with birth control pills. Being serious Christians, the answer was important to them. Being a Christian physician, I was quite concerned to practice according to biblical principles. The research that answered their question (and more) follows.

The practice of birth control is widespread because simple and effective methods are available. As we have seen, Christians may exercise stewardship over the size of their family within biblical parameters. This stewardship does not mean that all birth control methods are moral. Indeed, there is reason for the Christian to exercise caution concerning both the medical and moral aspects of birth control methods.

Birth Control Methods[64]

This review will omit discussion of both mild and severe side effects due to these methods. Also, omitted are those methods that clearly are abortifacient (that is, they cause the loss of the embryo or fetus after its conception) because they violate the biblical fact that life begins at conception. Thus, I will mention them only when necessary to describe their mode of action. Sterilization will be discussed separately because it is a more irreversible decision. The references by Potts and Hatcher provide much detail concerning each method. Comparative effectiveness will be discussed more fully in the next section.

Birth Control Pills. Birth control pills (or oral contraceptives) are a combination of two hormones (an estrogen and progestin) that are taken for 21 days of each menstrual cycle. Their mechanism is to suppress other hormones secreted from the brain (hypothalamus) that cause the maturation of eggs within follicles of the ovary and subsequent ovulation. Simply, ovulation is prevented, so no egg is available to be fertilized by sperm. If taken, they are almost 100 per cent effective, the only contraceptive (other than sterilization) that is. Limited to this mechanism, the morality of the use of birth control pills would be simple. Three factors, however, (discussed in the next section) warrant caution morally and medically in their use.

Condoms. The condom is effective to prevent sperm from being deposited into the vagina. In practice it has a high failure rate because "in the passion of the moment" it is not always used. Its unpopularity due to its decreased "sensitivity" for the man is offset by its less well-known tendency to prevent premature ejaculation and prolong erection. It is almost entirely without side effects.

Spermicides, Cervical Caps, and Diaphragms. Spermicides are chemicals that are placed into the vagina prior to intercourse to incapacitate or kill sperm before they can enter the uterus. They are commonly used with cervical caps that fit over the cervix or with diaphragms that fit between the pubis bone (the front part of the pelvis) and behind the cervix. These devices add a physical barrier for sperm as they attempt to enter the uterus. The effectiveness of the spermicide and the cap or diaphragm is enhanced by their being used together, but they are less effective than pills. Effectiveness, as with the use of the condom, has as much (or more) to do with its faithful use. Side effects are unusual and minor. There has been some concern that spermicides might cause birth defects but at this time the evidence is insufficient to advise that they not be used.

Withdrawal. Coitus interruptus is withdrawal of the penis prior to ejaculation. It is generally thought to be an ineffective means, but "the evidence contradicts this view"[65] It is at least as effective as spermicides and caps or diaphragms. Of course, the method requires considerable discipline by the man.

Breast Feeding. Lactation, or breast feeding, has a slight effect in preventing ovulation and thus preventing pregnancy. Nursing stimulates the production of a hormone (prolactin) that causes the breasts to produce milk and prevents the hormonal cycle that results in ovulation.

> Longitudinal studies of breast-feeding women suggest that ovulation practically never returns before some supplementary feeding is begun. Each month of breast-feeding adds approximately 0.3-0.6 months to the duration of anovulation.[66]

In countries where breast-feeding is widespread, pregnancies are spaced as widely as 3.5 years without any other form of contraception. (Other advantages and disadvantages of breast-feeding concerning the mother and her baby are not relevant here.)

Rhythm Method. Couples who use the rhythm method (periodic abstinence or fertility awareness) avoid sexual intercourse around the time that ovulation has occurred. As understanding of reproductive physiology has increased, this method has gained some sophistication with daily monitoring of the basal body temperature and cervical mucus. Its effectiveness is quite variable, depending upon the discipline of the couple and whether they use these additional monitors. It is generally as effective as sperm-icides, but strict discipline and the use of other means of birth control can make it much more effective.[67]

Abortifacients. 1) The intrauterine device (IUD or "loop") is a small device that is placed into the womb (uterus) through the opening of the cervix. It makes conditions within the uterus unfavorable to the implantation of the fertilized egg, so that it dies. 2) The "minipill" differs from the better known "birth control pills" in that it contains the progestin and not the estrogen. Its action is similar to that of the IUD in making conditions within the uterus unfavorable to implantation. Occasionally it does prevent ovulation but this mechanism varies from woman to woman and even from cycle to cycle within the same woman. Prevention of ovulation is not its primary means of contraception. 3) The progestin may be given as an injection every three months rather than being given in a pill, but the mechanism of action is the same as that of the "minipill." 4) The "morning after pill" is a very high dose of estrogen started within 72 hours after sexual intercourse and given daily for five days. Its mechanism is to make conditions unfavorable to implantation of the fertilized egg.

The Link between Birth Control and Abortion

What may surprise many Christians is the similarity of the thinking that surrounds birth control and abortion. This similarity, however, should not surprise because abortion is a major means of birth control. In light of the biblical argument to follow, this link is natural. Further, the common roots of birth control and abortion are apparent.

In 1922 at the First Birth Control Conference, racial preferences were expressed about the same time that Margaret Sanger advocated that "procreation of the diseased, the feeble-minded and the poor be stopped."[68] This slant towards eugenics continued in the 1920s and 1930s but, with the horror of Nazi Germany, the words were shifted to emphasize that a proper proportion of children should come from higher and lower socioeconomic classes. This rhetoric became

> an ideology of the common welfare which especially conforms to the conceptions of the upper classes as to what is necessary both for their own pursuit of happiness and for the kindest possible treatment of the multitudes of poor people crowding into public parks and drawing sustenance from Aid to Families with Dependent Children and other relief programs.[69]

This ideology is clearly the same as arguments for the current practice of abortion (and, it should be noted, euthanasia).

Francis Caravan has noted the similarity of the arguments for contraception presented in the late 1940s and early 1950s to those advanced in the mid-1960s for legalizing abortion:

> If anything is clear today, it is that the lowering of the barrier against contraception has been followed in a short time by demands for a more tolerant attitude toward abortion.[70]

Advocates portray the suffering of women who have too many children, children who are born badly deformed, and aged parents with various degrees of disability and pain. Then they call "barbaric and mindless" laws that do not allow for the needed remedies (abortion and euthanasia). Groups who oppose these remedies are called backward and non-progressive.

The euphemisms of contraception and abortion again show similarity. (It is to the shame of "pro-life" people that we use some of them as well). The possibility that a woman might become pregnant is a "fear of pregnancy;" a child that is not planned is an "unwanted child;" any woman has the "right to avoid pregnancy;" a child that does not fulfill all the parents' expectations (or amazingly survives an abortion) is a "wrongful birth;" a pregnancy that is not planned is an "accident;" and the decision whether to have a child or not involves "ambivalence." Christians even use the factory term, "reproduction," instead of the traditional Christian term, "procreation."

> Behold, children are a gift of the Lord;
> The fruit of the womb is a reward.
> Like arrows in the hand of a warrior,
> So are the children of one's youth.
> How blessed is the man whose quiver is full of them;
> They shall not be ashamed,
> When they speak with their enemies in the gate. (Psalm 127:3-5)

To continue to use the language of opponents is almost to lose the battle by default. Perhaps, even the words "birth control" could be changed to "stewardship of family size."

Almost all people who favor abortion, especially those associated with Planned Parenthood, will say contraception is preferable to abortion and that through more education and availability of contraceptives, eventually abortion will be unnecessary. This argument is specious. For the past fifteen years, millions of dollars have been spent on these programs and today abortions (1.5 million per year) continue at a staggering rate! Failure of contraception to obviate the need for abortion has been true in the past, also. In England, in 1949, those who used contraceptives had 8.7 times more abortions than those who did not.[71] In Sweden, government sanction of contraception resulted in a nine-fold increase in abortions from 1943 to 1951.[72]

> From data presented for countries in which contraception is
> already practiced by a substantial portion of the population, it ap-
> pears that permissive abortion laws may contribute more to a dim-
> inution of the effective practice of contraception than to a
> reduction in the birthrate beyond the level already established
> before the enactment of liberal abortion legislation.[73]

Unfortunately, the "planned" family concept has been virtually
adopted by evangelicals. For example, we are told a woman is
likely to get depressed when she finds herself pregnant subsequent
to the allotted one or two (children). She gets sympathy for her
"burden" from other Christians. When strangers find that she has
more than two children (especially if she has four or more) she
may be asked, "Are you Catholic?" That birth control should be
practiced is almost always assumed rather than the assumption that
children are a "blessing."

Moral Considerations of Birth Control Methods

Since the Bible does not proscribe birth control practices per
se, each method must be examined to determine whether a
Christian may use it. While categorically eliminating abortifacient
methods, (above), the overarching concern must be our attitude
toward the procreation of children. We must avoid the euphemisms of which we are guilty (Chapter 1) and return to the clear
biblical position that children are a blessing of God and that the
family is His basic unit of society. We must approach our
freedom to choose birth control measures with the attitude that if
a pregnancy occurs, it is not a burden that we bear, but that God
is exercising His Sovereignty to expand a family. The idea of an
"unwanted child" is entirely foreign to, and even condemned by,
the Bible. The presence of new life is *always* a cause to rejoice.
Consider Mrs. Tony Campolo. On certain social occasions she
may be asked by a woman who is a professional in some field of
study, "What is it that you do, my dear?" Such a question and the

manner in which it is asked, anticipates the reply, "I am (only) a
housewife and mother." Indeed, many Christian wives and mothers
view what they do as inferior. Not Mrs. Campolo. She answers.

> I am socializing two homo sapiens into the dominant values of the
> Judeo-Christian tradition in order that they might be instruments
> for the transformation of the social order into the teleologically
> prescribed utopia inherent in the eschaton.[74]

Usually, this shocks the other woman out of her demeaning
manner! Mrs. Campolo effectively communicates her godly and
supremely important role.

   Birth Control Pills. There are three possible moral objections
to birth control pills. First, even though the pills are completely
effective to prevent pregnancy, they do not always prevent ovulation. The frequency of this "breakthrough" ovulation ranges from
almost zero to ten percent of menstrual cycles according to the
strength of the estrogen and progestin used in each pill.[75] In these
instances conception could take place. It is, however, very unlikely
because changes have occurred in the cervical mucous that interfere with movement of sperm, in the ability of the sperm to
penetrate the egg, and in the transport of the egg through the
oviduct.
   We can roughly estimate the frequency of conception under
these conditions. Women in the child-bearing years without any
form of contraception will become pregnant at the rate of ten
percent per menstrual cycle. Women on the pill will ovulate in
four percent of their cycles (a rough average of all types of pills).
Multiplying ten percent times four percent, we have 0.4 percent
or one possible conception in 250 cycles (nine years). With the
combined effects of the various actions of the pills that interfere
with conception, it is likely that conception will be even less
frequent, *if it occurs at all*. Thus, the occurrence of conception on
the birth control pill is more theoretical than actual. Certainly, we

cannot say definitively that it does not occur. On that basis some Christians might object to the pill. My own position would be that the possibility of conception does not clearly make the use of the pill immoral. All the same the pill should be used only with the knowledge that conception and subsequent abortion is a theoretical possibility.

Second, serious side effects do occur. Most are related to the strength of the hormones themselves, so that the pills sometimes have to be stopped, exchanged for a weaker variety or ones with a different combination of the estrogen and progestin. In the past, physicians believed that the ability of women to conceive (become pregnant) is interfered with once the pills are stopped. Current evidence, however, indicates that the potential is slight, if it exists at all. Liver disease and high blood pressure are more common in women on the pill than those who aren't, but these problems usually resolve when the pill is discontinued. The most serious problems are an increased incidence of strokes, heart attacks, and blood clots (especially those that travel to the lungs and may cause death). Even so, the current data are not entirely clear. Further, even though morbidity and mortality may be increased, occurrences are rare.[76] Other side effects of these pills are less serious.

In favor of the pill is evidence that some diseases decrease or are prevented by their use: benign breast disease, ovarian cysts, ovarian cancer, iron-deficiency anemia, pelvic inflammatory disease, and ectopic pregnancy.[77] There is some *preliminary* evidence of reductions in rheumatoid arthritis and endometrial and ovarian cancers. Although it is impossible to say whether this set of benefits outweighs the side effects, the benefits do offset part of this second moral objection to the pill.

Third, the strongest objection to birth control pills is their interference with normal physiology. *Birth control pills* are among the few medications presented by physicians that intentionally interfere with normal physiology. Most medications and medical practices are directed at some abnormality or disease process.

These attempts to combat disease and disability are interferences with natural processes only in the sense that nature is fallen. They are without question consistent with biblical morality.[78] Birth control in general, and birth control pills in particular, then, are subjects of special moral concern to the practice of medicine because of their special effect.

Other forms of birth control do not involve the same degree of interference with the normal physiology of conception. With the rhythm method the decision whether or not to have sexual intercourse is a decision of the mind or will of the husband and wife. Although a husband or wife may not deny the other, both can agree to abstain at certain times (see Chapter 1). Thus, sexual intercourse is mostly a decision of their wills rather than an involuntary physiologic process.

At a purely physiologic level, other methods of birth control do interfere with the normal process of conception and pregnancy. But, other than the abortifacients already excluded, birth control pills most profoundly interfere with normal physiology, primarily because they interfere with physiologic (metabolic) processes within the body. The other methods prevent the union of the egg and sperm by superficial contact that is primarily external to the body itself. Paul Ramsey strongly states that "a vasectomy may be a far less serious invasion of nature than massive assault upon the woman's generative organism by means of contraceptive pills."[79]

If this interference with the normal physiology of the body did no harm, it would not be objectionable. Birth control pills, however, do have serious (even fatal) side effects (above). Since the body is the temple of the Holy Spirit,[80] it should not be intentionally harmed. In defense of birth control pills they seem to have some beneficial effects (above).[81] These beneficial effects offset the harmful side effects to some extent. The objection, then, is the degree to which birth control pills interfere with normal physiology, coupled with their harmful side effects.

We do not consider these three reasons sufficient to prohibit completely the use of birth control pills. They are, however, sufficiently serious that other methods are generally preferable, especially until a couple has the several children that they desire and where serious limitations to a family's size are not present (see Chapter 1). Apart from these moral problems there are some relative and absolute contraindications of birth control pills, for purely medical reasons, in some patients, that might preclude their use.

Continence and the Rhythm Method. Both the Old and the New Testaments instruct couples to abstain from sexual intercourse *in certain situations.* In the Old Testament these circumstances were uncleanness occasioned by menstruation (Lev. 15:19-28, 18:19, 20:18), a period following childbirth (Lev. 12:1-8), and religious reasons (Exodus 19:15, I Sam. 21:4-5).[82] Whether these practices are considered ceremonial, and therefore ended, or whether they were moral and should be continued, is a discussion that is too broad (and deep) to pursue here. Doubtless, these practices had a beneficial physical effect because God would not instruct His people to do anything harmful. Thus they should be continued for that reason.[83]

In the New Testament abstinence is possible for periods of prayer, but *both spouses must agree* (I Cor. 7:5). Paul does not say that abstinence cannot be agreed upon at other times, only that one can never deny the other. Since Christians are free to act in areas where action is not specifically prohibited, biblical instruction allows for the rhythm method as a method of birth control.

Coitus Interruptus. In Old Testament times *coitus interruptus* practice was the "most universal and commonly practiced" method by which pregnancy was prevented.[84] Onan avoided his levirate obligation in this way (see p. 98). Also, directions are given for the cleansing of a man who has had an emission of semen during intercourse or any other time (Lev. 15:16-18). If coitus interruptus were wrong, surely it would have been stated here. Further,

In the light of the fact that contraception was practiced by withdrawal, one would expect to find an express prohibition of the practice somewhere in the Bible if God considered it to be a sinful act in itself. But we do not find any such prohibition.[85]

Other Options. Those options that prevent conception and have relatively mild side effects are permissible: condoms, spermicides, cervical caps, and diaphragms. In addition, women must seriously consider breast feeding as a contraceptive measure, as well as for its intimate bonding effect between mother and baby. If a couple intends to have several children (and they should), then methods other than birth control pills are preferable. Let us look at the possible numbers. Without any birth control method, almost any fertile woman of child-bearing years will get pregnant within one year.[86] Yet, the condom, diaphragm (with spermicide) and cervical cap have a typical pregnancy rate at which a couple would have a child every ten years on the average. Surely, that is not too often! Spermicides alone have a pregnancy rate of one child every six years. Even the rhythm method would result in a child every four years. All these are "failure rates in typical users." Surely, with some discipline Christians could more closely approximate the "lowest observed failure rate."

Again, in this whole discussion the attitude that a child is a gift and a blessing of God is of the greatest importance. In that light a pregnancy is never a "failure" (of a birth control method) but a "success" in the eyes of God. We cannot entirely exclude birth control pills by biblical principle, but this method should be reserved for those uncommon instances when pregnancy *must* be prevented (see Chapter 1). In addition, Christians are not left to make these decisions; God has intended that the leaders of the church provide wisdom and counsel.[87]

The Physician, Birth Control, and the Single Woman

Linda had been coming to me for counseling for several months. Her recent life had been stressful. Her strained marriage had finally ended in divorce, leaving her with two teen-age boys and a young daughter. She had moved here from a distant city to be closer to her sister. I had talked with her sons because of their difficulty in adjusting to a new school situation. They occasionally threatened to go back to live with their father. Gradually, Linda's situation became more peaceful as the boys adapted and made friends and she began to become more disciplined in her day to day responsibilities. She remained unmarried.

I had also been her physician, helping her to sort out physical problems from symptoms that were psychosomatic due to stress. My involvement with her made her latest request more difficult and turned out to be her last request (of me). She wanted me to insert an intra-uterine device! Her reasoning behind this was a developing relationship with a man whom she had met and their "need" for sexual intimacy. In my own mind I wondered what I had really accomplished with her over the past several months. I told her that morally I would not do it. She never came to me again, as a physician or counselor. I later learned that she had seen another physician (who, ironically, also confessed to be a Christian) who did insert the IUD.

A common situation in today's practice of medicine is the prescription of birth control for single women of all ages. While you might expect the non-Christian to have little restraint in doing so, a Christian physician usually will comply, also. He may be strongly against abortion and abortifacients, but he will still comply. The reason usually given for this practice is that he is preventing the abortion of the pregnancy that may occur from "unprotected" intercourse. He will agree that sexual intercourse outside of marriage is immoral, but he sees this prescription as the lesser of evils. I contend, however, that such prescriptions are as serious and unbiblical as abortion.

First, the choice that this physician faces has been wrongly identified. His choice is not between two evils (see p. 14), but between his complicity in the *immediate* evil of sexual intercourse outside of marriage against only a *possible* pregnancy. Most sexually active teen-agers do not become pregnant. Of those that do, not all choose abortion, carrying the baby to term, keeping it, or allowing it to be placed for adoption. The pregnancy itself is certainly not an evil! (Consistent pro-life people even contend, rightly, for the pregnancy that results from rape or incest.)

Second, the biblical principle is clear that we cannot do evil in order to bring good (Rom. 3:8).[88] The evil here is most serious because the physician is an accomplice to a practice that violates the integrity of the family. The Bible clearly limits sexual intercourse to the family. Its practice outside of marriage is a denial of the procreation mandate, as well as one of the Ten Commandments. The violation of one commandment is as much a sin as the violation of any other. The violation of any one ultimately leads to death, both spiritually and physically. No matter how strongly a physician may protest, if he "gives in," he is guilty by his participation. The choice he makes is between pleasing God or pleasing his patient. The physician may tell the patient that he does not like what he is doing and he may even try to talk his patient out of her immorality. But if he gives in she will conclude that the issue was just not serious enough for the physician to resist finally.

Two commandments are violated if birth control is given to a dependent without the parents' knowledge (even though this practice is legal in every state). In this situation the violation of the Seventh Commandment is added to the violation of the Fifth. The latter is no less anti-life than the former. The Christian who practices this effectively destroys any argument for the biblical integrity of the family. Even when parental consent is given, that does not justify the practice of providing birth control to unwed teen-agers. No human authority has power to justify any sinful practice. A thorough discussion of birth control in minor girls, as it developed in England, but also from a biblical perspective is found elsewhere.

Third, to give birth control to unmarried women supports the liberal ethic that includes abortion, infanticide, and "neutral" sex education. Such prescription is an inconsistent witness against that philosophy. It is strange that a pro-life person is willing to practice even one tenet of that ethic.

Fourth, this practice separates a serious sin from its consequence. One deterrent to sin is a fear of its consequence, especially if one has experienced that consequence previously. This separation strengthens the notion that sexual intercourse outside of marriage is moral. A medical answer (birth control) has been given to a sociological (moral) problem. This same reasoning labels abortion "sound" medical practice. Somehow whatever is "medical" becomes moral. Another consequence of sin is removed when welfare payments are made to unwed mothers for their children. In many cases this income becomes a motive to have children. In these cases the state becomes a proactive accomplice.

Fifth, the woman may not be certain that she wants to engage in sexual intercourse and may not have already participated. The physician may be able to strengthen her will to resist, not uncommonly against unreasonable pressure from her boyfriend and peers. Less likely, but nevertheless possibly, the physician may convince her of the immorality of her choice.

Sixth, the abortion movement has demonstrated that what is deemed acceptable soon becomes mandatory. For example, some medical training programs will not accept students or residents who refuse to do abortions. Apart from successful resistance to the medical practice that grants birth control to unmarried women, the practice may also become mandatory for all physicians.

Already it is very doubtful, if not a foregone fact, that a pro-life physician or other health care worker would be hired by a state-owned college to work in its student health service where one of its major services is to provide birth control. Further, there has already been a court case in England in which a family physician refused to give birth control to the daughter of a family who was under his care.

Seventh, the physician assists his patients toward severe physical and personal consequences of fornication.   Over 20 bacterial, viral, chlamydial, mycoplasmal, parasitic and protozoan infections are now classified as "sexually transmitted." More are becoming known or are discovered to be transmitted in this way. Some are merely nuisances, others can recur for a lifetime, and still others can eventually cause death. Cancer of the cervix, for example, is now considered to be a sexually transmitted disease, associated with multiple sexual partners, intercourse at an early age, and a male partner who is promiscuous.

Any Christian physician who provides birth control measures for unmarried women must answer these objections *on a biblical basis*. Some Christians have come to see sexual immorality as a lesser evil than abortion.   The Bible does not support this position. In light of the above, one reviewer of this chapter asked, "What, then, do I do with these women? I need a rational answer to this question before I can reasonably consider your argument." My answer is, "The same thing that you do with patients who request abortion." (I know that he will not help any patient get an abortion, even refusing to give names of places or physicians who do them, but will try urge the patient not to carry out her plans and to seek alternatives.) He should do the same with unmarried women who ask for birth control. We must come to see that as disobedience to God the evil of fornication is no less an evil than abortion. (For a more thorough discussion of this subject, see references in the footnote.[89])

One distinction must be made. Birth control pills may be prescribed as medical treatment apart from the issue of birth control. For example, they can regulate the irregular and heavy menstrual periods that are common to teen-agers. Also, they can be used to control painful menstrual periods in women of all ages. In these cases a medical, not a moral, indication is present. Even so, where the patient is still a dependent, the parents should be made aware that birth control pills are being prescribed. Most teen-agers will not require such treatment, however, so this use of birth control pills is relatively infrequent.

Sterilization: The Procedures

Sterilization is a more serious step than the easily reversible means already presented. We will review the current procedures[90] and then examine the issue from a biblical perspective.

Male Sterilization: Vasectomy. Sperm develop within the testicles and upon ejaculation are carried via a small tube, (vas deferens), through the inguinal area, into the urethra, and out the penis. Vasectomy is simply the cutting and tying off of the vas deferens within the scrotum. Ejaculation still occurs but its contents will not have any sperm since the vas deferens is blocked. The distal portion of the vas deferens and the prostate gland may contain some sperm at the time of the surgery, so at least six weeks are necessary before one can rely on the ejaculate being free of sperm. The procedure is not invariably without failures, but they are rare.

Immediate complications of the surgery are rare and mostly concern the possible consequences of any minor surgery of a similar nature. Long term it was initially thought that vasectomized men had an increased rate of heart disease. Subsequent studies have shown that this concern is probably not valid. While some men may identify vasectomy with castration, serious problems occur only in those who were previously unstable.

Female Sterilization: Tubal Ligation. When the egg is expelled from the ovary, it moves into the Fallopian tube where it may be fertilized by sperm. Tubal ligation is the cutting and blocking of the tube to prevent sperm from reaching the egg. Although the basic procedure is the same, there are over 200 variations. For example, the surgical approach may be through the abdominal wall or through the vagina. Also, the tube may be cut and tied or cut and cauterized (burned with an electric probe). No method is invariably effective, but failures are rare. Hysterectomy (removal of the uterus) is certainly a form a sterilization but it is not considered acceptable medical practice when it is done only for the purpose of sterilization.

Immediate complications are more common and more serious than with vasectomies in men because tubal ligation requires entrance into the abdominal cavity where other structures can be injured. Major complications range from 3.7 to 31 per 1000 cases and a death rate of 1 in every 15,000 procedures. A long term complication may be a heavier duration and frequency of menstruation. Occasionally, women who have tubal ligations eventually require a hysterectomy for this reason. The same problems with self-identity may occur in the woman, as in the man following sterilization, but again are caused by previous instability.

Sterilization: A Biblical Perspective

It has been said with regard to sterilization as a form of contraception, that ". . . the decision . . . is correspondingly more momentous, but not fundamentally different."[91] I agree. One biblical passage, however, seems to indicate a more strict denial of sterilization, and needs to be discussed.

"No one who is emasculated, or has his organ cut off, shall enter the assembly of the Lord" (Dt. 23:1). Without question Calvin concludes that this person is one who has been castrated or otherwise had defective testicles.[92] That is, they were made eunuchs. Does their exclusion from the "assembly of the Lord," then, exclude sterilization altogether? I think not. First, this exclusion does not mean they could not otherwise be members of the state of Israel or counted among church members today. Neither Calvin nor Rushdoony considers that eunuchs were otherwise excluded from Israel. Calvin believes that this prohibition pertained to their not "communicating in the sacrifices."[93] Rushdoony believes that it pertained to their not holding a position of authority in Israel.[94] Both think the prohibition emphasizes the ultimate importance of holiness to all Israel. As such, it is one example among several others (Lev. 19:27, 28; Dt. 14:1).

Further support of this position is found in the fact that other prohibitions were not absolute either. For example, there was a prohibition against Moabites (Dt. 23:3), but the Moabitess Ruth became the ancestress of Jesus Christ (Ruth 1:4; Mt. 1:5). Thus, the prohibition of eunuchs pointed to one example of imperfection, among others, and not to sterility *per se.*

There is even a strong promise of blessing given to obedient (faithful) eunuchs (Is. 56:4,5). And, they could even become proselytes in a day of hardened Phariseeism (Acts 8:27, 28).

In the New Testament Jesus said, "there are also eunuchs who made themselves eunuchs for the sake of the kingdom of heaven (Mt. 19:12). From Paul's corresponding passage we know that Jesus was speaking of eunuchs in the sense that they would be sterile in that they did not marry (had the spiritual gift of celibacy) and not by voluntary castration (I Cor. 7:7, 32-34). In another passage this figurative sense is illustrated as Jesus moves momentarily from a literal to a figurative meaning (Mt. 5:28 to Mt. 5:29).

My conclusion, then, is that the procreation of children for believers is the norm and sterilization is the exception. Both may be consistent with God's ordering of His church. *Without specific limitations Christians are to obey the creation mandate.*

To those who have married and had children, Thielicke's caution against sterilization is appropriate. Likely, sterilization could not be considered until the couple has had three or more children or faced the permanent limitations of Chapter 1. Practically, one should also consider the possibility that he may lose his spouse, re-marry and desire additional children during their fertile years. Currently, the repair of vasectomies has a success rate (that is, a reversal that results in pregnancy) of 70 percent. The repair of tubal ligation has a success rate of 80 percent.[95]

Mandatory Sterilization

Three conditions have been used as grounds to justify mandatory sterilization: the mentally ill, the mentally retarded, and predictable genetic disorders. In the earlier part of this century

> major social ills–crime, prostitution, and poverty–were seen as stemming in large part from mental deficiency. This laid the groundwork for the eugenics movement based on the fear that the rapid, uncontrolled propagation of "mental defectives" would contaminate America's gene pool and eventually destroy civilization.[96]

Subsequently, laws were passed to force sterilization of these "defectives."[97] An example is North Carolina where sterilization may be authorized.

> because of a physical, mental, or nervous disease or deficiency which is not likely to materially improve, the person would probably be unable to care for a child or children; or, because the person would be likely, unless sterilized, to procreate a child or children which probably have serious physical, mental or nervous deficiencies."[98]

You should not overlook the breadth of this law. "Serious physical mental or nervous deficiencies" could cover any genetic disorder, so the law could be applied beyond the categories of the mentally ill and retarded. The law in its extreme could justify the sterilization of anti-government activists since these diagnoses often involve subjective criteria.[99]   North Carolina is not an isolated example; thirty states had similar laws for involuntary sterilization. David and Victoria Allen have revealed how some of these women understood what had been done to them, even avoiding marriage for that reason.[100]

Obviously, these laws were unjust. But should all of these people be allowed to reproduce without outside control? Even the Allens believe that the pendulum has swung too far in allowing the mentally retarded to have children.[101]

The issue is a difficult one. At the same time biblical principles do apply. First, you should realize that these categories are not entirely objective or "scientific." Problems in the diagnosis and management of so-called mental illness have been discussed elsewhere.[102] Mental retardation is perhaps more objective, but becomes less certain at the borders of intelligence where normal is separated from abnormal. Further, there are some valid criticisms of the methods of intelligence testing.[103] As to genetic disorders *every person* has several physical and mental aspects that could be better than they are. Thus, for all three categories the following discussion applies only to cases that do not fall into these gray zones. Those cases that are gray must receive scrutiny from the additional perspective of valid categorization.

Second, very few genetic disorders affect all of the children born to a particular couple. This creates is a real dilemma. The only way to detect a genetic abnormality is after conception, implantation, and some growth of the embryo. Then, the only option to prevent the birth is abortion, an unbiblical alternative. The Christian couple, then, must decide *before they conceive* to accept the child born to them. We have reviewed some considerations for couples who have a high likelihood of genetically "defective" children in the previous chapter.

Third, the state never has the right to govern procreation. God gave the command to the family. The opposite side of this command is the responsibility of the family, not the state, to provide for its own, primarily, with the church as an additional resource. This responsibility of the family includes any "defective" children.

Fourth, and perhaps the most crucial factor, eugenics is the predominant reason for sterilizing persons falling into these three categories. As we will develop in a subsequent chapter, any consideration of eugenics (as separate from genetic engineering) in the planning of offspring is wrong. Thus, any grounds for sterilization must be justified on other grounds. A corollary of this principle is that there is nothing immoral in the procreation of "defective" children. That is, couples are not morally obligated to avoid having such children.

Fifth, no unmarried mentally retarded person should ever be without a "parent" in the biblical sense. The concept of legal guardian does not qualify because this designation only requires that legal matters are kept in order, not necessarily parental oversight. In most instances the "parent" should be the natural parents. Where they are not, the person who has this role should have the personal interest, involvement, and total responsibility that parents have for their children. This role, however, should not limit the maximum freedom ("normalization") that the mentally retarded person can achieve. For example, normalization could include living outside the parent's home in a "community living arrangement."[104] When two people who are mentally retarded marry, then they must "leave" their parents and "cleave" to each other (see Chapter 2). Of course, their parents should be available when asked for help, but by this biblical instruction they must be freed from parental control to make their own decisions.

With these principles in mind let us look at what I believe to be the three most difficult situations in which sterilization might be necessary. The first situation (two mentally retarded people who marry and have children) continues our discussion from the paragraph above. Would they be competent as parents? Would they be able to train children properly and provide for them? Would their children with normal intelligence be able to "out-smart" their parents, causing them to lose control of the home?

Obviously, where one spouse has normal intelligence, the situation would be no different from any other marriage. Since ninety percent of the marriages of retarded people are in this category; we discuss here the exception rather than the rule.[105]

The concern over the ability of the latter to raise children is erroneous. First, the few studies available indicate that they function about as well as "normal" parents.[106] Any limitations seem to be related to socioeconomic status (another slippery criterion at best) rather than to intelligence. Second, the children themselves are not likely to be limited in their intellectual development because of a phenomenon called "regression to the mean." That is, the genetic trait of intelligence is not an average of their parents, but a "regression" (really progression) above the parents' intelligence toward the average of the population. (This phenomenon is also present in those with very high IQs and would then be a "regression.") In fact, the mean IQ of children born to parents who are both mentally retarded is 74. Third, many parents of normal, even high, intelligence, are inadequate parents. So, intelligence alone does not determine who are good parents. From a biblical perspective the best parents are those who raise their children in the "nurture and admonition of the Lord" (Eph. 6:4b KJV). The mentally retarded can be quite capable of this.

Another situation involves the mentally retarded person who is sexually aggressive. First, the problem rarely occurs. The mentally retarded are sexual offenders no more often than others.[107] When it does occur, the mentally retarded person should be treated under the law as any other offender. Even though he may understand less about right and wrong (this lack of understanding should not be assumed), he is still a danger to the public. Sterilization in the form of a vasectomy, will not affect his sexual aggression. Castration would, but its consideration takes us into another area of morality that is beyond our discussion of sterilization. Perhaps, in some cases castration might be the best alternative for the mentally retarded person where the only other option is strict isolation in an institution, but all other alternatives should be considered before this one. It is likely that castration would rarely be necessary. The likelihood of abuse, however, must always be guarded against because "hard cases" do not make for "good" (normative) ethics.

The final situation concerns mentally retarded persons who are vulnerable to sexual exploitation because their mental retardation prevents their understanding of proper sexual relationships, including their inability to ward off the sexual advances of others (not necessarily others who are retarded). The person might live with his or her parents, in an institution, or in a community living arrangement. Of course, every precaution should be taken to prevent any situations where such abuse could take place. We should understand, however, that 24-hour monitoring (however desirable as a goal) is a practical impossibility. The final decision, however, to sterilize is that of the parent(s), not the institution or the state. We have seen previously that the creation mandate was given to married couples. This authority may not be usurped by the state.

None of these conditions change any biblical principles to justify sterilization. I find it difficult, however, to be dogmatic. Today, few sterilizations on the mentally retarded are performed on an involuntary basis and all women over the age of eighteen must have judicial approval.[108] Although I have maintained that this decision must finally be made by the parents, our legal system does not always agree with biblical principles. Where we can we must make every effort to see that practices are biblically consistent and not just legal.[109]

The "mentally ill" are governed by the same principles as the mentally retarded except that the considerable overlap of moral responsibility with mental inability requires even more scrutiny of the "mentally ill" than mentally retarded. In most instances where the person is incapable of normal function because of an organic etiology (identifiable physical or biochemical abnormality), mental retardation will be the cause.

The long distance call came Saturday night when complex ethical dilemmas were far from my mind. The young husband on the phone and his wife, however, had spent many agonizing hours over their decision and were seeking biblical counsel. Their problem was their inability to conceive a child. They had been married for several years and were considering artificial insemination by donor (AID). Investigation by several doctors had revealed that they would be unable to conceive children by any means using the husband's semen, so their doctors suggested AID and were surprised at the couple's reluctance to accept it. The couple were not sure that this procedure was biblically permissable and wisely were seeking counsel from others (not just myself).

They caught me off balance! I had never done any serious investigation of the biblical principles concerning artificial insemination. I told them that my present answers were tentative, but I would investigate the matter further, using their call as a stimulus. The following content of this chapter is my answer. We will present the procedure and then consider it biblically.

Artificial Insemination: The Procedure[110]

More than fifteen percent of all married couples are infertile. One method to overcome this problem is artificial insemination.

Sperm, obtained by masturbation, is placed into the vagina or uterus to enhance its chance for union with the egg released from the woman's ovary. Sperm of the husband (AIH) or sperm from a donor (AID) may be used. In previous years sperm from one or more donors were sometimes combined with sperm of the husband (CAIH) or sperm from several donors were combined (CAI). Now, the procedure is almost entirely limited to the use of one donor at a time. (More than one donor, however, may be used over time as the procedure usually must be carried out several times before conception occurs.) AIH is rarely performed today because problems that interfere with the deposit of sperm through intercourse also limit its use for artificial insemination. These problems are a low sperm count, retrograde ejaculation (sperm are propelled backward rather than forward due to some anatomical abnormality) and conditions in the vagina that injure the sperm. Spiritual problems that prevent conception are non-organic impotence in the man, frigidity in the woman, and the homosexual orientation of the man or woman. These problems of infertility may be corrected with AIH.

A new technique that washes the toxic, but naturally occurring, chemicals from the semen, concentrates it, and places it directly into the uterus has the potential to increase the use of AIH. That procedure, however, is not likely to become widespread because of the ready availability and acceptablity of AID. For Christians who believe, as we do, that AID is wrong, the AIH technique does provide a new alternative. Experience with the technique is still limited but initial results are promising.

Artificial insemination, however, has expanded beyond the initial reasons for its use. This development was to be expected, since technology in modern times seems to have few moral limitations. In a survey of the practice of artificial insemination (the first survey of this type) ninety-five per cent of the physicians who performed AID, did it for infertility of the husband.[111] Thirty-three percent inseminated women because the couple feared transmission of a genetic disease through the husband. (These diseases were Rh incompatibility, cystic fibrosis, diabetes, hemophilia, Huntington's disease, muscular dystrophy, and Tay-Sachs disease.) Almost ten percent of the practitioners had carried out the procedure for single women! Although this article did not mention lesbians *per se*, it is likely that some of these inseminations for single women included partners of lesbian couples. (Some ethicists . . . have actually argued for the morality of artificially inseminating lesbians.[112])

Artificial insemination has become quite common. About 172,000 women had this procedure in 1987 performed by 11,000 physicians. Some 65,000 children were "reproduced" with 30,000 being conceived with sperm by AID. Since the procedure was first introduced, the number of children born of this procedure is approaching one million!

Artificial Insemination by the Husband

AIH is morally acceptable when the procedure is simply a technical by-pass of the cause of the failure of the sperm of the husband to unite with the egg of his wife. On this basis almost all ethicists and religious bodies (except the Roman Catholic Church) argue that AIH is morally permissable.[113] There are some aspects that may be immoral. First, it is difficult for masturbation not to be sinful because it almost always involves sexual fantasy and may involve the use of pornography. Such lustful thoughts are adulterous (Mt. 5:27-28). A better approach might be to have the husband and wife make the collection of sperm a part of their sexual encounter. The sperm could be collected in a condom and immediately transferred to another container, even making masturbation unnecessary. Special precautions may be necessary to insure that no chemicals are present on the condom to damage the sperm, so particular directions from the physician who is managing the infertility problem must be followed closely.

Second, the couple's marital relationship should be evaluated, especially if there is not an obvious physical problem or admitted impotence of the man or frigidity of the woman. This evaluation and counseling, if necessary, should be carried out by a Christian who is trained and experienced in biblical marriage counseling; preferably a leader from the couple's own church.[114] Biblically, a case cannot be made for withholding AIH because marriage problems exist, since there are no biblical criteria to be met before children may be conceived (other than marriage itself). The church, however, should counsel the couple separate from the need for AIH. Not to be overlooked, either, is the possibility that sexual intercourse may be quite infrequent, not taking place but every few weeks or months! In my counseling I am amazed at the infrequency of sexual intercourse among some Christian couples. Although this infrequency almost always stems from other problems in the marriage, it gives opportunity to temptation (I Cor. 7:5). Such infrequency of intercourse may actually be *the cause* of the infertility.

Failure of Christians to understand the biblical concept of marriage (Chapter One) may be expressed relative to AIH: "We need a child to complete our marriage." Such a statement makes a mockery of the concept of the marriages of those couples who will always be childless and those whose children have left home after growing up. A marriage is complete *without children*. A couple has children because it is a commandment (Gen. 1:28) and a blessing of God (Ps. 127:3-5) as His design for the raising and evangelization of children. Certainly, children add a dimension to marriage that otherwise does not exist but they are not necessary for the fullness and richness of the biblical purpose of marriage.

Some may question the morality of AIH because it is "unnatural." This objection needs little attention because *all* that physicians do is an "unnatural" interference with the "natural" course of morbidity and mortality. Not only is this design true of medicine, but practically all that man does is against the relentless deterioration and destruction in the world. We turn on the heat when it gets cold and go indoors when it rains. Man's "life is one constant intervention in nature . . . ."[115]

This intervention, however, does not morally allow a couple to store sperm "in case something happens." For example, a husband may be sent to war and the couple desires to be able to have a child if he is killed. Thielicke's argument is that AIH "cannot be a security measure against threatening 'possibilities.'"[116] That is, the soldier's death is only a possibility, not a certainty. It is impossible to guard against all the possible contingencies in this life. Hope in all circumstances is assured by God's promises to His people, not our own attempt to cover all eventualities (Rom. 8:28). Further, legal problems may develop as to the ownership of the sperm and, if the husband is killed, the wife may decide to remarry rather than use the sperm. If she doesn't remarry, is it right for her to raise a fatherless child? This situation is an example where the violation of one moral principle makes it impossible to govern the resulting situation by moral principles. Whatever one does is wrong. The couple must rest in God's plan for them whether or not it is His will to bring them back together.

Artificial Insemination by Donor

AID, as either CAI or AIHD, is morally more complex than AIH and is not consistent with biblical teaching. The most serious objection is an intrusion into the unity ("one flesh" relationship) of the husband and the wife. Helmut Thielicke calls this a "psycho-physical unity."[117] We have discussed already the biblical concept of this unity (Chapter 1). Only one further point should be made about Thielicke's term. Psyche in New Testament Greek designates the soul, the immaterial component of man.[118] Union of the souls of the husband and wife does not occur since in the after-life they are no longer husband and wife (Mt. 22:23-33;

Rom. 7:1-3). Thus, "psycho-physical unity" refers to the functional
unity of companionship and work, not the union of their souls.

AID breaks this unity and is significant to the extent that
another person (the conceived child) may result.

> When one understands the "one flesh" concept in marriage as a
> holy sexual unity, from which, in normal situations and at certain
> times, new individuals may find their beginnings, then the active
> insinuation of another individual's active genetic potential and
> personal history into that unity seems to be disruptive. The
> woman is now engaged with someone else (anonymously and
> sexlessly) in bringing a new life into that unity. The female part
> of carrying, and delivering one whom God ordains to be naturallly
> the result of the unity . . . . When one of the partners uses his
> or her individual portion of the one-flesh sexuality to "father" or
> "mother" a new individual outside of their particular male-female
> unity, it seems to me, in that instance, to be destroying the
> one-flesh concept of that partnership.[119]

Further, the woman has a biological inheritance in the child and
the man does not: that is, " . . . the fulfillment of motherhood is
not accompanied by the fulfillment of fatherhood."[120]   This inequality is not present with adoption because both share equally
as the child becomes a member of their family and both nurture
it. Neither is involved biologically, but both are involved functionally. Both are subjected to the blessings and trials of child-raising.
With AID, however, the husband does not have an equal identity
with his wife to the child. The frailties and sinfulness (to which
we are all subject) may prevent the same attachment and care by
the husband as his wife.

CAI is likely to present the greatest problem since either (or
both) the husband and the wife will continually wonder if it was
the husband's sperm that fertilized the egg, and they will never
know for sure. Through elaborate genetic mapping it is possible
to be certain, but the very quest to have this typing done reveals

deep-seated anxiety. Further, this mapping is not widely available (yet) and would doubtfully be done for this purpose.

I will allow that this inequality may present little apparent problem to a family. Three objections, however, are still present. First and foremost, an inequality has been introduced. That the problem of this inequality is overcome (at least functionally) does not prove that moral choices were made. Biblical principle, not experience (pragmatism), is always the test of morality. The Bible does not allow for this inequality, especially coupled with all the potential problems with donor screening. Second, it is arrogant to predict that you will perform well in a situation to which you have not yet been exposed. In this case neither the husband nor the wife is able to predict how they will handle the presence of the child.

Third, the fact that problems rarely occur in those families with AID children[121] illustrates that the present understanding of marriage is limited entirely to biological considerations. This focus is consistent with the materialism (as a philosophy) of our age and denies the primary biblical purpose of marriage; companionship and cooperation. It equates marriage with the sexual relationship.

There are other serious objections to AID. The most serious is adultery. Some Protestants readily dismiss adultery as an issue with AID. Although Christ's words are clear that adultery can be committed in one's heart (Mt. 5:27-28), adultery otherwise includes physical contact. It is not convincing to say that the presence of a substance from the sexual organs of another man, obtained by a sexual act, and placed within the sexual organs of a woman who is not his wife, does not constitute adultery. Certainly, this whole procedure is mostly technical, largely separated from the passion that accompanies adultery. Virtually all Protestants agree, however, that an individual person is a unity (regardless of the combinations of body, soul and spirit that are argued). As a unity, the substances (egg and sperm) that procreate life cannot be easily separated from the non-material element (spirit or soul) of persons.

Important to this discussion is the moral significance of semen. Semen *per se* is not just bodily tissue. The potential that it has to unite with an egg to procreate a person with an eternal soul is unique. Even if the soul of this new person is not present until conception,[122] the genes within the sperm carry personal characteristics of the biological father. In this sense, the person of the biological father is present in the sperm. Thus, AID is more than an introduction of a biological component of man. It carries representations of the person of the biological father. This personal element brings AID even closer to a definition of adultery.

Although masturbation by the donor may possibly be performed without adulterous thoughts, that is highly unlikely. The recipient woman is not as likely to have adulterous thoughts toward the donor, but she may. The fact that most donors are young (frequently medical students), and that local papers run pictures of handsome men to attract donors, increases her temptation.

A greater problem exists with the thoughts of the donor. The use of pornography as an aid to masturbation has been unashamedly acknowledged in a recent article on reproductive issues.[123] The donor may also direct his thoughts to the unknown woman recipient. Knowing the sexual preoccupation and permissiveness of our society, it seems impossible that the semen could have been collected without adulterous thoughts during masturbation by the donor.

Thus, *adultery is not easily dismissed.* All these associations are perilously close to adultery, if it is not actually present. Semen is not easily separated from some kind of lustful thought, nor is it easily separated from the persons of the donor and recipient: "a sexual act (semen obtained by masturbation) has been interposed between the husband and the wife."[124]

Some biblical accounts are relevant and often mentioned when Christians discuss reproductive issues. Even though God had promised Abraham that Sarai would bear him a son (Gen. 15:4), Sarai convinced Abraham not to trust God's promise and to take matters into his own hands. Thus, he conceived Ishmael by Hagar, Sarai's Egyptian maid (Gen. 16:1-4). God did not honor Ishmael as Abraham's heir (Gen. 17:18-21). That is, He did not honor the violation of His spoken word in Abraham's attempt to circumvent Sarai's (current) inability to bear children. Further, the Ishmaelites became one of the many peoples in the Middle East who were (and are) the enemies of Israel (Ps. 83:6). Although this account involves adultery, it also involves an attempt to bypass the procreative process between husband and wife. In this instance, adultery is not condemned by God and He honors His previous promise to give Abraham and Sarai a son, Isaac.

God will fulfill His promise that truly Christian marriages will be full and complete *with or without children*. The decision for or against AID is the same decision that Abraham and Sarai faced: to trust God for His plan of blessing or attempt to circumvent their circumstances in their own way. If children are part of God's plan for a particular couple, then God will provide them. If children are not in His plan, then He will still fulfill his promises for the fullness that a marriage can have "in Him." They may also realistically continue to hope for children because childless couples have children almost as often as those who are helped to reproduce medically (see later in the chapter).

Lot's daughters, fearing the unavailability of men by whom to have children, seduced their father. The children born to them were the progenitors of the Moabites and Ammonites who were perpetual enemies of Israel (Gen. 19:31-38). Tamar is another example of a person who chose to procreate in an immoral manner and disgraced her family in the process (Gen. 38). We can only conclude from these accounts that man's circumvention of God's revealed design for procreation results in tragic consequences; a warning for us today. (God's provision of children through the Levirate and kinsman-redeemer arrangements is discussed in the next chapter.)

The next objection involves eugenics, that is, the selection of desired characteristics for the expected offspring, another way of saying that one person (with certain characteristics) is more valuable than another (the utilitarian ethic). This topic will be dealt with more fully when discussing genetic engineering, but it applies here. Potential donors must be of a certain age (21-30), blood type, social standing and intelligence. Admittedly, these criteria do not approach the attempts to select Nobel Laureate winners (see below), but they involve eugenics nevertheless.

The opposite danger is too little control over who donates. Most of the more than twenty sexually transmitted diseases (STD) can be transmitted through semen to infect the mother and the conceived child.[125] Her husband could also be infected before the STD is manifested or detected in the woman. One STD, acquired immuneodeficiency syndrome (AIDS), is always fatal and is becoming more prevalent:

> screening procedures for the detection of these agents in donor semen have not been standardized . . . . The use of fresh semen (rather than frozen semen that can be more adequately tested) is clearly hazardous and should be discouraged.[126]

> The screening of donors for genetic diseases was woefully inadequate . . . . Current practices reflect little concern for consanguinous [see following] matings or other effects of multiple donor use . . . . Present records on artificial insemination are woefully deficient . . . . information concerning artificial insemination is scanty.[127]

These reasons alone ought to discourage anyone from seeking AID. Also, donors could be on some drug or have some physical problem that could lead to genetic malformation. Clearly, any removal of responsiblity for the contraction of diseases is opposed to the integrity of Christian marriage

> People are operating on blind faith (in an amoral medical system) . . . when they trust the heredity of their children to commercial sperm banks.[128]

An episode that made national attention illustrates such degradation, immorality, and the lack of controls. The Repository for Germinal Choice is the sperm-bank that selects only "geniuses" as its donors. Its first child was born to parents who were "convicted Federal felons" (actually paroled from prison) and "who had lost custody (of their children) from a previous marriage after allegations of child abuse" that included beating the children with a strap, sending one "to school in pajamas with a sign proclaiming him a bed wetter" and pasting "the word 'Dummy'" on another.[129]
Whether this sperm-bank and others are more careful in the future does not detract from this graphic illustration of what can happen when the sanctity that should surround the procreation of life is controlled by agencies outside the family.
The next objection is consanguinity, that is, conception between close relatives where there is a greater risk of genetic defects because defective genes may be paired to cause a defect or malformation that might be otherwise mildly expressed, if at all. The Old Testament explicitly restricts such marriages (Lev. 18:6-18, 20:10-21; Deut. 22:30, 27:15-26). Geneticists differ, however, on the degree to which such kinship should be extended.[130] A close relative of the donor may be the recipient of such sperm, totally unknown to either donor or recipient. Admittedly, this danger is small, but some programs use the same donor from fifteen to fifty times and several half-sib matings have nearly occurred already.[131] The greater danger is that the children born by this procedure may later marry each other because sperm donors commonly donate

repeatedly. If the recipients are located in the same geographical area as the donors, such a marriage is more likely.

My next objection is the commercial degradation of sacred areas of life. Although profit in and of itself is not immoral, it easily degenerates where profit is pursued to the neglect of other values. The deficiencies with sperm banks are likely motivated by the profit motive. Certainly, the donor's personal psychophysical unity is brought into question. He is really a "seller" not a "donor":

> this vision of a (medical) student working his way through college is not without an element of the macabre and gruesome . . . . (this system) presupposes an existential disease, namely, a pathological divorce between the physiological and the personal dimension of the sex realm . . . . the sex process becomes anonymous and impersonal."[132]

The role of abortion, another manifestation of our immoral culture and legal system cannot be overlooked relative to AID. Adoption formerly was the moral alternative to AID. Today, adoption is quite difficult, if not impossible, because abortions kill almost 1.5 million babies each year. Obviously, they are unwanted (an understatement!), so all could be made available for adoption and likely be sufficient to supply all childless couples who wanted them. Thus, the prevalent need for AID *is directly* related to the problem of abortion. Immorality breeds immorality and one immoral practice is developed to "rescue" us from the tragic results of another.

Legal difficulties may not directly correspond to biblical standards but legal confusion about AID is another reason to object. Both American states and foreign countries have inconsistent and conflicting laws, if they have any at all.[133] To review what has been enacted would require a complex review since the laws vary widely. Instead, I will pose some sample legal questions.

Whose name is to be filled out as the father of the child on the birth certificate? If the child is "defective" in some way, who is liable for the cost of its medical care: the biological father, the woman who bears the child (including her husband), the donor bank, the obstetrician, or the state? Who is the legal owner of the sperm: the donor or the donor bank? Should a woman be impregnated without her husband's consent? (Such a possibility is real where a woman is legally able to abort her unborn child without her husband's consent.) In Ohio one medical school program has already been ordered by a U.S. District judge not to exclude single women from its artificial insemination program.[134]

One cannot be sure that current laws will continue to prevent the conceived children from tracking the identity of their biological fathers. In California one person conceived by artificial insemination has already won her case.[135] In Sweden legislation is being considered to allow the children born by AID to obtain the names and addresses of their biological fathers or any information that may lead to their identity and location.[136] With the strange (by comparison to traditional values) legal and judicial decisions that are enacted today, it is possible that visiting rights or financial responsibility might be given to the donor at some point. Fortunately, in the United States infertility clinics mostly restrict their clients to married couples. We believe that the complexity and inconsistency of laws and judicial decisions reflects the immorality of the procedure: *where God's law is transgressed man is not able to construct consistent, workable laws.*

Infertility, Suffering and Faith

Perhaps I have seemed insensitive to the plight of the childless couple, erecting barriers to a simple reproductive method that is readily available. I have not, however, intentionally sought to burden anyone. I do seek the biblical balance of love and truth. Love without truth is unguided sentimentalism; truth without love is the right direction administered with iron gloves. John and Sylvia Regenmorter and Joe McIlhaney have written a compassionate book on reproductive issues. We highly recommend that book to balance any lack of compassion perceived here.[137] Our only disagreement with them is their approval (even though hesitant) of AID. With almost all other issues we are fully in agreement. Those couples with children, particularly, should be sensitive to those who have been unable to have them. As we have seen, childless couples are quite numerous and found within churches and Christian groups.

Regarding the problem of infertility, Helmut Thielicke says that we "dare not contradict the meaning of suffering."[138] He *is not* saying that the infertile couple must accept their situation without any effort toward conception or adoption. He is, however, emphasizing the lack of willingness among modern Christians to accept their God-given lot, albeit different from what they personally desire. Too often, biblical principles are compromised where deep feelings cause one to conclude, "Surely, a loving God would not allow this situation to continue." The difficulty of a situation *never* determines biblical principle. In Christian history and modern situations it is quite clear that God does not avoid severe trials for His people. If the biblically-allowable procedures do not result in a child, then childless couples should praise God for His plan for them.

> "For My thoughts are not your thoughts, Neither are my ways your ways," declares the Lord" (Isaiah 55:8).
> "All discipline for the moment seems not to be joyful, but sorrowful; yet to those who have been trained by it, afterwards it yields the peaceful fruit of righteousness" (Heb. 12:11).

The Bible also issues this warning:

> "There are three things that will not be satisfied,
> Four that will not say, 'Enough:'

Sheol, and the barren womb,
Earth that is never satisfied with water,
And fire that never says, 'Enough'" (Prov. 30:15b-16).

This passage underscores the strong, driving impulse behind the desire of a childless woman to conceive. Examples (previously given) include Lot's daughters, Tamar, and Abraham.

Further, we must remember that the primary purpose of marriage is fully attainable for every Christian couple. The suffering of childlessness may be one means that God uses to further that fullness.[139] Paradoxically, the couple must be careful that their infertility does not prevent this primary purpose from being achieved. Man's sinful nature is such that even the desire for motherhood can become inordinate.

The strongest plea put forward in defence of AID is the plight of those married women who long for children but whose husbands are sterile. Repeatedly it is said – by such women and on their behalf – that what they need and desire above all else is to have a "child of their own." "Nothing else in the world will satisfy them." We need not affirm once more the profound compassion which this frustration must evoke; but our concern at this point is to answer the question whether such a desire – one which impels a wife to become the mother of a child who is not her husband's, but some other and unknown father's – is in strict truth inordinate: one which exceeds the proper (righteous) bounds of desire. There are some whose sexual impulses might be similarly described; but that is not defence in a court of law, nor, we suppose, in the eyes of the public at large. We are all, without distinction, required to restrain our desires, however imperious. On what rational ground is it urged that while sexual desires ought not to be indulged at will, parental desires may be? And are the results of indulgence later likely to be quite different, in their total effect on the personality, from those which are known to follow in the former? If we persuade ourselves that because we want a thing so much it must be right for us to have it, do we not thereby reject in principle, though perhaps unwittingly, the very idea of limitation,

acceptance, of a given natural (Biblical) order and social frame –
in a word, of the creatureliness of man?[140]

Medical Limitations

On a practical level, medical science is actually not very
effective with infertile couples. First, eventual pregnancy is only
slightly enhanced by medical science. One study shows pregnancy
occurring in 41 percent of treated couples and 35 percent occurring in untreated couples, a difference of only 6 percent.[141] The
study considers all types of infertility problems, not just those
involving artificial insemination. Thus, the exact numbers of those
who chose this procedure cannot be extracted. In one category,
however, where artificial insemination might be used, 60 percent
of the pregnancies occurred in untreated couples.

Second, there is serious question whether studies of semen
have any relevance to the likelihood of eventual pregnancy.[142] The
characteristics of semen from couples who remained infertile were
virtually the same as the semen in those couples who eventually
conceived. (Both sets of couples were being followed in the same
infertility clinic.) Third, no good evidence shows that any medical
or surgical treatment can significantly increase either the number
of sperm or those characteristics of the sperm that are supposed
to enhance their chances of fertilizing an egg.[143]

The large portion of this chapter has discussed the moral issues relative to artificial insemination. Here, we have briefly
reviewed the real limitations of medical science. This limitation
is an excellent example of the false dichotomy that Christians and
other ethicists face. That is, *the efficacy of the medical approach
being ethically considered is assumed,* when the real situation quite
often is that medical science has little to offer.

This false assumption is, perhaps, the greatest limitation to a
truly biblical-medical ethic. I have discussed this lack of efficacy
at length.[144] If a medical approach is questionably efficacious, then

any ethical argument to defend and promote it is itself unethical. Yet, ethicists argue at length, often compromising both biblical truth and Western tradition, to justify a method that does little, if anything, to improve either the health of individuals or society. If Bible-believing Christians could grasp this one principle, an application of other principles to concrete reality would be facilitated.

Conclusion

In this situation and all situations the childless couple must be certain that what they do is permissible for " . . . whatever is not from faith is sin" (Rom. 14:23). Counsel should be sought from wise and experienced Christians, preferably within their church leadership. If such counsel is not available, one wonders why they remain in that church since the church is God's means by which believers are matured in their ministry to each other (Eph. 4:11-13).[145] Our prayers and concern, as well as this biblical instruction, go out to couples who must work through this very difficult situation.

CHAPTER 4

IN VITRO FERTILIZATION

Robin and Arthur had been married for fifteen years and were still without a child. She had had two emotionally painful miscarriages after which they had decided not to try to have children again for seven years. Then, they became aware of the possibility of *in vitro* fertilization. The procedure was explained to them and they were told to think it over. After several months they believed themselves to be ready to try the procedure.

> We knew we were taking a gamble. But you do it because its offered to you, it's an opportunity, it's part of the program of becoming pregnant, and we felt that maybe it would work for us – we'd be the lucky ones who beat the odds. If you don't think you're going to beat the odds you don't do this. You really have to believe it's going to work.

Unfortunately, after several attempts at the procedure Robin was still not pregnant. They had spent $25,000 without a successful pregnancy. Now, they are considering adoption but they face the long waiting lists of adoption agencies.[146]

Artificial insemination places sperm within a woman artificially to impregnate her. The sites of impregnation and fertilization are the same as those that occur from intercourse. *In vitro* fertiliza-

tion (IVF), however, involves the manipulation of the egg as well
as the sperm, and some of the subsequent events of the pregnancy
itself.[147]

Before proceeding, some basic issues should be reviewed. 1)
All principles relating to artificial insemination apply here. 2) All
principles that apply to abortion apply to IVF (see below).[148] 3)
Results of sinful practices, such as sexually transmitted diseases
(formerly called venereal diseases) and induced abortion, have
contributed to the wide-spread interest in IVF. 4) Eugenics may
be an overt or covert motive in IVF. 5) Scientism, the belief that
science provides the ultimate truth and determines its own
morality in man's quest to extend his knowledge and dominance
over nature, is a prevalent attitude among IVF researchers. 6)
Modern desire to have sexual relationships without the responsibility inherent in such intimacy and according to biblical design
has contributed to interest in IVF. We will first review the
technique, then proceed to a biblical analysis.

In Vivo and In Vitro Fertilization

In vitro is Latin for "in glass." In science it designates those
procedures with living tissues that are performed outside the total
organism in an artificial environment (that may or may not be
glass containers *per se*). *In vivo* refers to a process that takes
place within the total living organism. "Fertilization" is the
successful penetration by one sperm (occasionally more than one
sperm in multiple pregnancies, such as twins) into the egg of the
woman with subsequent division (cleavage) of the fertilized egg
into two cells and then repetitive divisions until differentiation and
completion of the various organ systems take place over the
following nine months. Sperm reach the egg by traveling from the
woman's vagina (where they are deposited by sexual intercourse)
through her uterus and Fallopian tubes where conception occurs.
The fertilized egg (conceptus or zygote) then is propelled back

down the Fallopian tube to become implanted into the uterus some 4-6 days later. Thus, the embryo exists for several days *before* it becomes implanted into its mother's womb.

In vitro fertilization is indicated when dysfunction or blockage of the Fallopian tubes prevents sperm from reaching the egg, or the egg after it is fertilized from reaching the uterus. There are various reasons for this dysfunction or blockage, but the most common cause is gonorrhea, a sexually transmitted disease.

In vitro fertilization begins with the collection of eggs from the woman just prior to the expulsion of the egg from the ovary (ovulation). Matured eggs form a bulge on the surface of the ovary where they can be seen by a lighted scope and retrieved through the abdominal wall. Since the egg is 1/125 inch in diameter, it cannot be found after ovarian rupture has occurred. Thus, retrieval must occur after eggs have matured, but before the cyst (within which they develop) ruptures. Special hormones are used to stimulate maturation of the eggs so that several eggs may be "harvested." Up to 17 may be obtained, but the usual number is 5-6.

The semen from the man and the egg(s) from the woman are placed in a Petri dish containing a special medium that will provide nourishment and left for 18 hours. Usually, several of the eggs become fertilized and start to cleave (divide). By definition the conceptus after the first division is called a blastocyst or embryo. After 48-72 hours in the Petri dish the 2-4 cell embryo is transferred to the woman's uterus. Since ovulation was not allowed to occur, she is given hormones to prepare the uterus for implantation. The embryo or embyos is (are) placed into the uterus where it is hoped that they will become implanted. Two weeks of waiting begins: if menses occurs, the egg(s) did not implant; if menses does not occur, it (they) did implant and the pregnancy has begun. The wait is not over, however, because one-third of IVF pregnancies spontaneously abort within the first three months. The rate of success – in the development of a full term infant – averages 10-15 percent among centers that have reported their results.[149]

One advantage of IVF is the reduced number (50,000-100,000) of sperm necessary compared with *in vivo* fertilization (30 million). Thus, a low sperm count, one cause of infertility, may be managed by IVF. As with artificial insemination, donor sperm can be obtained from sperm banks in those cases where the quality of the husband's sperm is inadequate. "Egg banks," like sperm banks, have been considered but the current trend seems to be toward frozen embryos or "embryo banks" (see below).

Gamete intrafallopian transfer (GIFT) is another possibility in special cases. In this procedure the sperm and the eggs are placed in the end of the fallopian tube that is farthest away from the uterus. Thus, fertilization takes place *in vivo*. It is interesting that the Catholic church has approved this procedure where the sperm is collected in a special condom, a portion of the sperm is placed in the vagina, and the sperm and the eggs are placed into the fallopian tube via separate transfer catheters (so that fertilization cannot possibly take place outside the woman's body).

Possible Combinations. 1) A woman may be artificially inseminated, the conceptus washed out before it implants and placed into another woman. 2) A woman could be artificially inseminated with the sperm from a man to whom she would give the child when it was born, a type of "surrogate" mothering. 3) An embryo, resulting from the union of an egg and sperm from a couple who were not able to conceive, could be implanted into another woman who could carry the child until it was born, and then turn it over to the biological parents. Using various combinations of donors and surrogate mothers, there are 10 or more different ways to "reproduce."

The cost of IVF is from $3500 to $6000 *per* procedure, depending upon the center where it is performed. With a 10-15 percent "success" rate, the cost per live birth would range from

$20,000 to $60,000. It was estimated that over 3000 babies have been born worldwide by this procedure.[150]

Sin As a Cause for IVF

It is estimated that more than one in six couples in the United States is infertile and more than a million seek help for this problem from doctors and clinics each year. Several hundred clinics throughout the world perform IVF. At first glance it seems that these clinics provide a much-needed service. This perception is only partially true, however, as many causes of infertility are sin-related. When reviewing these causes, however, remember that a significant number of causes are not sin-related.

Two extremes should be avoided. First, to call all infertility the direct result of personal sin. Second, to say all infertility is something that occurs naturally and cannot be related to personal responsibility. My belief is that too little attention has been given to the second factor. Infertile couples seem to be "lumped" together as a group of guiltless "victims." Sin does have consequences, as we will see. Unfortunately, the exact numbers that fall into the following categories are not known, but without question they constitute the more common causes of infertility.

Sexually Transmitted Diseases (STDs). Within the last twenty years the number of infertile cases has tripled.

> Doctors place much of the blame for the epidemic on liberalized sexual attitudes, which in women have led to an increasing occurrence of genital infections . . . (that) scar the delicate tissues of the fallopian tubes, ovaries and uterus.[151]

Dr. King Holmes, a university professor, has stated, "the greatest potential for any decrease in infertility is in the prevention of sexually transmitted diseases."[152] The simplest and most effective prevention is God's ordained pattern within marriage. (Of course, he did not mention that method of prevention.)

Too often discussions about abortion and infertility do not go back to the beginning of the problem, but start with the consequences that occasion concern. Each person reaps what he or she sows (Gal. 6:7-8). Pastors, doctors and counselors should inquire about such origins. The infertile Christian couple who now sits in front of you wanting a child may be the victims of their own previous immorality and are now trying to have a child by any means available. This previous sin will need to be acknowledged and confessed. Other couples will be guiltless and no confession of sin will be necessary. All situations require sensitivity by the counselors. The goal is not to provoke guilt, but to analyze and counsel according to a biblical understanding of the situation. Comforting the couple for their infertility is not always the *only* pastoral concern.

STDs cause spontaneous abortions, as well. To quote Dr. Holmes again, "STDs contribute to more embryo wastage than is currently appreciated or understood."[153] STDs cause conditions in the Fallopian tube that may allow sperm to pass through and fertilize the egg but the fertilized egg cannot pass through to the uterus for implantation. In this case an embryo will implant in the abdomen (abdominal pregnancy) or in the open part of the tube (tubal pregnancy), very rarely resulting in a live birth (and then only by Caesarian section. Usually, severe bleeding occurs and the embryo must be removed surgically to prevent the woman from bleeding to death. Spontaneous abortions from STDs are also caused from inflammation of the wall of the uterus because implantation is prevented. In this case the woman will likely never have any awareness of being pregnant.

Abortion. The need for IVF is increased because of the lack of babies available for adoption. If abortion was not possible, all babies (1.5 million per year) would not be placed for adoption, but the number would almost certainly be sufficient to provide children for infertile couples. Thus, adoption could eliminate the need of IVF altogether, if infertile couples were content to have children in this way.

Postponed childbearing. The older a couple is when they attempt to have children, the more likely that complications may prevent conception or that their child may be born with physical problems (see Chapter 1). The average time it takes for a woman over 35 years of age to conceive is two years, as opposed to six months for younger women.[154]

Scientism. "Scientism" denotes the attitude that there is no area of knowledge that should not be investigated with the tools of science and that "what can be done should be performed" without consideration for its morality or immorality. The following are some examples of this attitude relative to IVF.

1) After reviewing the positions of the British and Australian research councils on IVF research, one author stated, "The need for such guidelines is great, in order to allow knowledge to progress."[155] Note his ultimate concern: not morality or side effects in the mother and baby, but "knowledge." His concern represents an attitude prevalent in the medical literature.

2) Scientists proceed without restrictions. Normally, before a procedure is practiced on humans, it is extensively tested in animals. Such prior testing was *not carried out with IVF.* "This (IVF) is one American medical technology that has grown up backwards."[156] When a federal moratorium was called on IVF in humans, animal experimentation was continued. Then, after successes in England and elsewhere, IVF was begun *on humans.* Especially desirable would have been the long term follow-up of animals conceived by IVF to determine their normality. Paul Ramsey contends that this reason alone is sufficient to ban IVF.[157] This followup in animals has never been carried out.[158]

3) Scientists ignore their own warnings. Dr. R.G. Edwards whose work resulted in the birth of Louise Brown (the first baby born from an IVF conception) is an example. In one article he gave fifteen pages of assurance that there was no risk of deformity

from IVF.[159] But then, he spent four pages warning all participants that they may be legally liable for "wrongful life."
Ramsey was "stunned by this contradiction in a single article by an
eminent scientist."[160]

But that isn't all. Dr. Edwards stated in the same article that
there was a need to avoid publicity concerning IVF to allow the
child to grow up normally, as any other child. When Louise
Brown was born, however, the event was broadcast around the
world![161] This reversal is evidence that scientists are quite willing
to violate their own standards of "morality" whenever they please.
The "drivenness" of such scientists (whatever their motives),
causing them to ignore almost all restraints, should not be
underestimated.[162]

Consequences of Abortion. Induced abortion, especially when
done more than once, can cause physical problems that make
fertilization more difficult or prevent it altogether. Also, the guilt
and anxiety that often result from abortion can cause impotence
or frigidity as a cause of infertility.

Misunderstanding of the Concept of Marriage. In the biblical
concept of marriage children are not the central or permanent
dimension of marriage. Much of the "demand" for artificial means
of conception comes from the distortion that children are required
to complete or fulfill a marriage.

Conclusions. These situations demonstrate that *the "boom"
demand for IVF is very largely a result of the evil of our day.* As we
consider the morality of IVF we must not ignore the fact that the
consequences of sin bring sin. Sowing produces a harvest greater
than that which was sown; one seed produces much fruit.

The Status of the Embryo and Fetus

Perhaps the greatest objection to IVF, as commonly
practiced, is the fate of the embryo or fetus. Usually, more than
one egg is fertilized to enhance the possiblity that one will be

"normal." The biblical position[163] is that individual human life begins at conception (fertilization). So, failure to implant *all* fertilized eggs into the uterus results in the destruction of human life. Researchers justify this destruction on the basis (1) that some fertilized eggs are obviously deformed as they are viewed through the microscope and (2) that some embryos may be frozen and saved for another attempt at IVF if the present one is not successful. Biblically, however, innocent human life must never be destroyed.

Second, the current rate for successful IVF averages only 10-15 percent (above). Thus, the great majority of embryos are never born. This figure is not very high, but you should also realize that in "normal" couples 31 percent of all fertilized eggs that implant in the uterus undergo spontaneous abortion (miscarriage).[164] Those that are lost before implantation are estimated to be a similar number.

Biblically, what can we say about the embryonic and fetal waste that occurs in IVF when it also occurs naturally? Considering the restrictions that follow, and stating absolutely that all eggs fertilized *"in vitro"* should be placed into the woman's uterus, this rate of loss cannot be used as an argument against IVF. My restrictions, however, are not consistent with most IVF protocols. Thus, such changes in the usual protocol for IVF would be necessary to meet biblical criteria.[165]

Third, amniocentesis and the "preventive measure of elective abortion" are standard procedure.[166] Amniocentesis makes it possible to detect genetic abnormalities for which the "solution" is induced abortion. To be consistent, those who are against induced abortion on biblical grounds must be against amniocentesis in IVF as well.

Fourth, embryo and fetal experimentations are usually performed without the regard due human life. Since 1975 in the United States a moratorium by the Ethics Advisory Board (EAB, see following) of the former Department of Health, Education, and Welfare has prevented federal funding for such experimentation. This moratorium has effectively prevented IVF experimentation under private grants as well.   Researchers want this moratorium lifted.[167] In some countries experiments have been carried out. But even there, the moral climate requires that they be circumspect in what they do. Indeed, the atrocities of the past, under the name of research, warn us of what is potentially possible here.   Christians must demand that the embryo and fetus be treated consistent with their status as a person.

The controversy about experimentation on prenatal life has brought up the relevant problem of the inability of the embryo or fetus to give its consent. Two protests are voiced by Leon Kass and Hans Tiefel respectively:

> One cannot ethically choose for a child the unknown hazards that he must face, and simultaneously choose to give him life in which to face them.

> No one has the moral right to endanger a child while there is yet the option of whether the child shall come into existence. That is the crucial and decisive argument against the clinical use of *in vitro* fertilization.[168]

These ethicists have not, however, considered the risks to which all parents expose their children, both *in utero* and thereafter, and the biblical responsibility of parents to make those decisions.

Perhaps, IVF brings into clearer focus the awesome responsibility of all parents who contemplate bringing a new human life into existence.   The hazards of gestation alone are staggering: genetic malformation that may occur as the sperm and egg unite and further divide to differentiate tissues and organs; the complications of pregnancy, such as eclampsia (very high blood pressure with the possiblity of convulsions in the mother leading to the death of herself and her baby) and the difficulty of childbirth.

After birth, the child faces the risks of disease, injury and other trials.

So, in spite of ethicists' concern, all parents assume responsibilities for their future children. These ethicists' concerns, however, do underscore the fact that serious thought and prayer should precede the conception of a child – a neglect of which most of us are guilty. Further, such responsibilities clearly show the callous disregard for human life conceived by fornication or adultery.

The ethicists do not consider that God has given, even commanded, that married couples assume this responsibility for their children both before and after birth. The biblical basis for responsibility has been reviewed elsewhere.[169] Suffice it to say here, that parental consent to conceive and make all decisions relative to the health of their unborn and born children is God-given. The concern of these ethicists may reflect the modern error that gives children the right to make their own decisions, sometimes over their parents' decisions. This encroachment into God-given responsibilities within the family is already legal for many medical practices,[170] but must be condemned as unbiblical, destructive to the family unit, and ultimately dishonoring to God. He made such family responsibilities analgous to the relationships within the Trinity (John 5:30, 8:28, 15:10; I Cor. 11:3).

Experimentation and Freezing of Embryos

Most scientists do not give the embryo biblical status.[171] In fact, its status is still being debated. The Ethics Advisory Board (EAB) of the former Department of Health, Education and Welfare did nothing to resolve the issue when they "attempted to steer a course between the extreme positions of the embryo having no status as a 'human subject in any morally relevant sense' and the view that at the moment of conception, a person exists with full rights of protection under the law."[172] As a result, they established:

> 1) that any research involving the human embryo have as its intent the establishment of the safety and efficacy of eventual implantation . . . and 2) that no embryos would be "sustained *in vitro* beyond the stage normally associated with the completion of implantation (14 days after fertilization)."[173]

Although the board failed to say that human life begins at conception, fortunately its actions do restrict fetal experimentation to very limited instances. Pro-life Christians should thank God that the EAB set such precedents and has (at least for the time being) prevented the atrocity of fetal experimentation in the United States.

When "scientists" face moral constraints upon their technologies, however, they may re-define terms to lessen or remove moral restraint. Accordingly, the embryo was given a new subdivision, the "preembryo," that is, "a product of gametic union from fertilization to the appearance of the embryonic axis" [about fourteen days after fertilization]" . . . *[it] is not a person* but [is] to be treated with special respect because it is a genetically unique, a living human entity that might become a person[174]" (my emphasis). In light of the procedures that *are* performed on the "preembryo" (below), it is difficult to see that any more respect is given to it than to living human tissue (for example, that which may be handled during surgery). Thus, researchers and clinicians may virtually do anything with the "preembryo." I will not use "preembryo" because I do not recognize any such spiritual distinction.

By contrast the Bible clearly states that life begins at conception when it says, "she conceived and gave birth" (Gen. 4:1,17; 21:2; Ex. 2:2; etc.) This unity of conception and birth in these instances involve persons called by name. So any experimentation after conception must consider that it involves a real person.

One exception, often cited, is the occurrence of monozygotic twins. Dizogotic twins (twice as common as monozygotic twins) result from the fertilization and implantation of two eggs simultaneously.[175] Monozygotic twins result from division of the fertilized ovum sometime shortly after conception (within 8 days). If division occurs after this time, conjoined (Siamese) twins result. Since the fertilized ovum in monozygotic twins contains what will become two or more persons (triplets and other multiples may occur by this same mechanism), it is argued that individual human life does not begin at conception. This argument is specious. Since at least one individual life will result from fertilization, the embryo still must be treated as a person. The fact that we cannot predict or detect that more than one individual will develop does not detract from the fact that at least one individual *already exists*. Such an argument is one more example of attempts to develop ethical principles from rare exceptions.[176]

In their efforts to improve the IVF success rate researchers have begun to use cryopreservation (freezing) of embryos. This technique offers several advantages. Extra oocytes can be collected at the time of aspiration of the ovaries and fertilized. Those not used in the initial transfer into the woman can be frozen and used later, if a successful pregnancy does not result. Thus, the woman does not need to undergo as many laparoscopies. In addition the woman will not need hormonal stimulation for future attempts (to "mature" the oocytes), avoiding those side effects that cause the uterus to be less susceptible for the implantation of the embryo. Frozen embryos can also be used to impregnate other women.

Freezing of embryos must be severely condemned. Any advantages are abrogated by the clear immorality of the procedure. Since individual human life begins at conception, the embryo must be regarded commensurate with that status. If people are frozen for future use, what happens to them if that use later becomes unnecessary? For example, the woman may become pregnant and not want another child. Further, 40 percent of frozen embryos are "damaged irreparably" (that is, to interpret this euphemism, they die).[177] Such destruction of life is inconsistent with biblical sanctity of life.

Even if freezing were perfected in animals so that there was no possible harm to the embryos, the status of the person as the embryo is still too precarious. Neither local, national, nor international courts or legislatures have been able to make or pass consistent laws. Further, the embryo is exposed unnecessarily to an *in vitro* accident, such as the loss of electricity to the freezer or exposure to some noxious agent. Those restricted instances in which IVF is moral, are possible *without* the freezing of embryos.

The dangers are illustrated by a real case in Australia in which embryos were frozen, only to have both parents die in an airplane accident. That the courts faced a dilemma over what to do with these embryos demonstrates their failure to see the embryos as "real" people. The courts viewed them as property to be given to someone, not persons who should have legal rights similar to those of minor children.

A Morally-Acceptable Situation

IVF may be morally acceptable if: 1) The sperm and the egg are obtained from a man and woman who are married to each other; 2) all embryos are implanted into the woman's uterus; 3) induced abortion is not an option (unless the life of the mother is endangered by the continual pregnancies); and 4) amniocentesis is not an option except for therapeutic reasons that endanger the life of the fetus. These conditions preserve the psychophysical unity of the husband and wife, the integrity of the family, and the sanctity of the life of the unborn child.

Some Christians believe the brief *in vitro* period violates the sanctity of the reproductive process. They may desire a ban of IVF altogether. If I had to choose between their position and the current almost limitless use of this technology, then their position is a better choice. Indeed, some credence can be given to their position by the fact that the *in vitro* period could possibly injure the physical status or well-being of the embryo. My position, however, is not to reject technology itself, but to structure biblical limits and proscribe only if clearly warranted.

EUGENICS: Eugenics both overtly and covertly is present in IVF. We have already reviewed the selection process regarding the use of donors for sperm (Chapter 3). Since IVF often involves donated sperm, what was said in that chapter applies here and to the egg donor as well. Also, surrogate mothers may be chosen for qualities that are desired by the couple who will receive the child. When we focus on eugenics specifically (Chapters 5, 6, and 8), we will see that those principles apply here.

Surrogate Mothers, Artificial Wombs and the Adoption of Embryos

Jane Williams was going to have her own baby! Who would have thought it possible for a woman whose womb had been removed more than twelve years earlier. Actually, she was not pregnant, but her friend, Nancy Parks, was the surrogate mother who carried the genetic child of Jane and her husband. The menstrual cycles of the two women had been synchronized to allow eggs to be taken from Jane's ovaries, fertilized with her husband's sperm *in vitro* and the embryo transferred to Nancy's womb. After five months everything was proceeding "normally," although perhaps not naturally.[178]

Using various combinations, a baby can have five "parents." An egg from one woman (1) is fertilized *in vitro* with sperm from one man (2). The embryo is then implanted into the uterus of another woman (3) and carried until the baby is delivered. Then, the baby could be adopted by another man (4) and woman (5). (If they divorce or are widowed, there is the possibility of more parents!)

As we will see, not all the people in this process are true parents. Nevertheless, the complexity of family identity brought on by IVF is vividly demonstrated.

DEFINITION OF A PARENT: Before we can examine the morality of surrogate mothers, we must determine from Scripture what a parent is. First, parents bring children up "in the discipline and instruction of the Lord" (Eph. 6:4; more detail is found in Dt. 6:4-9). Although spiritual training is primary, such education is total, including vocational training.[179] Old Testament laws, history, and Proverbs, in particular, give us a complete picture of this education.[180] Second, a parent provides for the physical needs of his children without which they are considered as one who " . . . has denied the faith, and is worse than an unbeliever" (I Tim. 5:8). Third, parents are to provide an inheritance for their children (II Cor. 12:14).[181] Of course, the most valuable inheritance is the total training that they receive rather than physical property.

ADOPTION: Fourth, parents normally procreate their own children. God's primary provision for the procreation of children is through biblical marriage. This criterion, however, is not an absolute prerequisite for parenthood. Adoption is an alternative that provides a means by which children become full members of the family, legally and socially. What is required from the biological parent(s) is their full release of all privileges and responsibilities of parenthood. On this basis the modern trend to allow adopted children to know and meet their biological parents is unbiblical.

The authoritative model is God's adoption of believers, " . . . the right (authority) to become children of God" (Jn. 1:12).[182] God is the perfect Parent, fulfilling all the above requirements: total instruction (II Tim. 3:16-17), total provision (Mt. 6:25-34; Phil. 4:19), an amazing inheritance (Eph. 1:18-23), and even the spiritual equivalent of genetics, the presence of the Holy Spirit

(II Cor. 2:22, Eph. 1:13). Parenthood clearly does not require that children be biologically-derived. Many cultures, including that of the Roman Empire within which Paul wrote, have had a biblically-acceptable concept.[183]

This biblical concept of parenthood prohibits surrogate mothers. A woman who is pregnant qualifies as a parent by the criteria we have presented. Throughout her pregnancy she cares for the unborn child in the foods and medications that she takes in (or fails to take in) and her attitudes will profoundly affect the child.

Our laws even recognize the right of inheritance of the child within her womb. It is not the fact of birth that establishes this right, but the presence of the child within the womb. Further, only the death of the child prior to its birth cancels this right, as it does at the death of any other family member. If the surrogate mother provided the egg that was fertilized, the child also has her biological inheritance.

At first glance it may not be apparent that the mother is providing discipline and instruction. Such a conclusion, however, is premature. The baby experiences cycles of sleep and activity. It is aware of emotion and human voices and is reassured by the mother's heartbeat. Even the father contributes to this environment as his relationship and interaction with the mother is the strongest and most continual influence in her life. Some might be sceptical about this "education" of the unborn child, but extensive research reveals the sensitivity of the embryo and fetus to such stimuli.

This interaction between a mother and her unborn baby may account for what has been labelled "maternal-fetal bonding." That is, a mother has a strong attachment for her infant even at the moment of its birth. Those who plan to release their babies for adoption find it hard to give them up. The same has been true of surrogate mothers who find "that they must build an emotional wall of separation between themselves and the tiny humans they are carrying . . . . they must harden themselves not to become involved . . . ."[184]

The motives of surrogate mothers are often immoral.[185] The primary motive is monetary, with more than forty percent unemployed or on welfare. Others enjoy being pregnant without the responsibility to raise the child. Some try to absolve guilt brought on by previous abortions. Certainly, some surrogate mothers could have altruistic motives, so this reason is not absolute. It would seem, however, that a surrogate mother's claims of altruism are questionnable unless they serve without remuneration except for expenses incurred by their pregnancy!

Another problem is that either "parent" could back out of the contract. In one case the parents to whom the child was to be delivered refused to accept it. When problems developed during delivery, these "parents" refused to accept the "damaged goods."[186] The surrogate mother might also decide to keep the baby. The contracting parents might die, leaving a mother with a baby she can ill afford and against whom she had steeled herself to avoid bonding. Laws at the state, national and international levels are inconsistent and ambiguous concerning who has what "rights" to this contractual "product of conception."

ARTIFICIAL WOMBS: The above interaction between a mother and her unborn child shows why biblical principles prohibit the use of artificial wombs. Social isolation experiments that have been done on monkeys show that profound problems develop.[187] Although these experiments occurred after birth, effects prior to birth can be extrapolated. Considering the rapidity of changes in the womb and strong maternal-fetal bonding, the effects on the unborn could be greater. Such experimental evidence is never needed to corroborate biblical principles,[188] but research that does agree suggests that right biblical interpretations have been made. Although "total external development of the entire embryo, has neither been carried out nor seriously set as an objective,"[189] artificial wombs will probably be proposed and even attempted.

Any use of wombs in animals for human embryos or fetuses must be condemned absolutely. God made all things after their kind (Gen. 1:21-25). Such an abomination is far worse than surrogate human mothers, but this method of prenatal nurture has been seriously proposed.[190]

ADOPT AN EMBRYO: From the biblical limitation of conception to married couples, someone might propose that the embryo from a married woman could be washed from her uterus and placed into the uterus of another married woman; that is, adoption at conception! This proposal, however, is not so morally plausible as it might appear. The purpose of adoption is making legitimate that which is illegitimate, both legally, socially, and spiritually. For an embryo that is conceived legitimately, the criterion for adoption does not apply. There is no biblical warrant for the procreation of children specifically for the purpose of making them available for adoption. Embryo adoption must also be rejected because it poses a hazard to the embryo that would not otherwise exist. The embryo may fail to implant after transfer to the other woman and die. Any unnecessary risk to human life is unjustifiable. There is also the complicating factor that the embryo may still implant in the donor's uterus if it is missed in the wash-out technique. Then, she has a "problem" pregnancy to resolve.

The Kinsman-Redeemer and The Levirate

In discussions of alternatives for childless women, Old Testament references (Deut. 25:5-10) to the kinsman-redeemer and the levirate are relevant. Their purpose is the continuation of the family name and the retention of family property. The marriage of those "related by blood or by marriage, marriage and sexual

union by a widow or a widower to in-laws was considered incest
– except in this one instance."[191]   If a woman's husband died
without children, she was permitted "to marry her next of kin in
order to raise up a family to bear the name of the dead man"
(Dt. 25:7).   It was Onan's responsibility to marry Tamar to
continue the name and property of his brother, Er (Gen. 38:8-10).
His sin was his failure to impregnate her because he "wasted his
seed on the ground." Tamar's subsequent act to seduce her father
was a desperate act of a woman who desired children from the
same stock as her husband and *not* a fulfillment of the levirate
obligation.

The other example of this situation in the Old Testament is
the account of Ruth and Boaz. Since she did not have a brother-
in-law to act as a levirate (Ruth 1:11-12), the responsibility fell to
the "kinsman-redeemer," her closest relative.   In this case the
"close relative" (unnamed in the biblical account) passed his
responsibility to Boaz, the next closest relative to Ruth.

Concerning IVF, does it seem that these exceptions could
allow for continuance of the family name and property? The
answer is a definite, no! First, these special circumstances called
for actual *marriage* of those involved, preserving the psycho-
physical unity of marriage and its procreation of children. We
have already demonstrated that both AI and IVF are restricted by
biblical principles to married couples. The introduction of sperm
or egg from outside the marriage violates this unity. Second, the
levirate and kinsman-redeemer are the only exceptions to the
procreation of children outside the norm for families in the entire
Bible.   Exceptions to God's Word are never our prerogative.
"Only He can modify his own directives for His good purposes."[192]

Risks to the Mother and Child

Louise Brown can in no way have a natural human life. If she is
not psychologically damaged from her beginning, socio-psychological

ruin seems invited. If she is Britain's best   tennis player at Wimbledon or if she becomes a juvenile deliquent, the outcome will be explained or excused by the child's unique genesis.[193]

Thus, Dr. Paul Ramsey argues against IVF because of its potential effects on the conceived child. Certainly, IVF takes place in an artificial environment. Hormones are used to stimulate the development of eggs within the ovary (with some not being fully mature). Fertilization and the early divisions of the embryo are *in vitro* and in the presence of chemicals to which it is not normally exposed. Additional hormones may be used to assist the retention of the embryo-fetus. The mother has intense emotions during the whole experience.

The risks to the mother are less, but not insignificant. She must have general anesthesia (i.e., be "put to sleep" in an operating room) for the laparoscopic extraction of her eggs.   This anesthesia poses rare but real possibilities for permanent damage to various organs of her body and even death (extremely rare). Transfer of the fertilized egg into her uterus has little risk. The pregnancy itself probably has no more risk than a "natural" pregnancy, assuming that amniocentesis and Caesarian section are not routinely planned for the pregnancy.[194] The hormones that may be used to assist in the prevention of premature loss of the fetus have little risk and are often used in other pregnancies that repeatedly end prematurely.

The risks to the mother are justifiable because all medical interventions and all pregnancies involve some risk.   Where my previous restrictions are enforced, the desire of the husband and wife to have children warrant these risks.

The risks to the child are not as easily accepted – if at all. Further, the risks to the future offspring of these children must be considered. The major problem is *that we do not know* what they may be. Although there is a higher rate of spontaneous abortion in the first trimester following IVF than in naturally-occurring pregnancies, the children who are carried to completion of pregnancy do not seem to have any more problems than one would expect by natural pregnancies. The IVF protocols that call for induced abortion of fetuses who show certain abnormalities (thus eliminating many present and future problems with these children), however, is unacceptable.

There are two reasons why these risks to the fetus do not proscribe IVF. First, practical experience does not seem to support this concern. It is well-documented that most severe genetic defects in embryos and fetuses end in spontaneous abortion. Some mechanism seems to recognize such abnormalties and cause them to abort. This process functions as a "natural" screen for genetic disorders. Some abnormalities survive, but they are severe in less than one percent of pregnancies. Second, medications are a routine part of medical practice and pose some risk of genetic malformations to present and future generations. If these medications are morally acceptable with regard to this potential, it would be inconsistent to restrict IVF without clear evidence of an increased incidence of such problems.

The several thousand pregnancies of IVF add to our assurance that these risks are acceptable. That experimentation continued in a reckless manner does not justify its having been done, but the knowledge available should not be ignored. The risks to the mother and to the future child seem no greater or worse than any medical procedure involving reproduction. Diligence must be maintained, however, to detect any preliminary evidence that excessive harm may occur in the future.

Summary

I have argued for IVF in those cases in which both the sperm and the egg come from a man and woman who are married. According to biblical principles, *all* embryos must be transferred into the woman's uterus, and amniocentesis and induced abortion must routinely be omitted from the IVF protocol.

Even so, I have led you through a labyrinth of possibilities that could make this procedure immoral and unbiblical. They are summarized, as follows (without respect to degree of importance). 1) The procreation of human life is too sacred to be manipulated to the extent that it is in IVF. 2) Effects may be produced that do not show up for a generation or more. 3) The embryo in its critical stage of development should not be isolated from the human body of its mother. 4) IVF, as well as AID, involves a "ladder of unnaturalness" that moves towards further abominations, such as eugenics and cloning.[195] 5) What is acceptable can become law. That is, the immoralities of IVF may eventually become a legal right, as has happened with abortion. 6) No society today has sufficient moral standards to restrict this procedure according to biblical principles. 7) Funds used for this procedure could be used for other types of medical care. Certainly, third party payments or governmental grants should not be used to fund IVF.[196] 8) This procedure did not receive the extensive testing that usually preceeds the treatment of humans. 9) An argument can be made that IVF is not a medical procedure.[197] 10) This procedure came about largely as a result of other personal and societal sins, as reviewed above. 11) There is evidence that the motives of many participants in IVF are excessive, and thus, immoral.

I consider these possibilities sufficiently serious to conclude that the better route is to avoid the procedure entirely. At the same time I do not believe that any one factor, or all together, are sufficient to prohibit the procedure when carried out according to biblical principles. Each Christian will have to weigh these possiblities in prayer, study, and meditation for his answer before God and with the counsel of his church leaders.

CHAPTER 5

GENETIC ENGINEERING: I

Mark and I became friends through our mutual interest in high school sports. As far as I knew, he was an only child. He had never mentioned another brother or sister. I had visited his house on several occasions, but had not seen other children. One visit, however, revealed someone else. I do not remember if this visit was unexpected or if Mark's family knew me better and were less vigilant. Walking through their kitchen, I saw a girl lying on the floor on a pallet in such an awkward position that she appeared to be a distorted assembly of thin legs and arms with a head randomly placed somewhere among them. I was so startled that I merely glanced and went on without a word. On another occasion she appeared in a similar position in the back seat of their car. Eventually, I asked about her. Briefly Mark said that she was his sister and that she had been that way all her life. After that exchange we never discussed her again. That day in their kitchen became indelibly fixed in my memory. She was my first exposure to the grotesque deformity that can occur from genetic problems.

Genetic engineering, like no other subject, brings us close to the extremes of the scientific and the biblical understanding of man. Any discussion of these areas can quickly move into deep water. The attempt, however, is both worthwhile and necessary. It is worthwhile because all ethics in general, and medical ethics in particular, are closely dependent upon the anthropology (view of man) upon which they are based. Discussion is necessary because genetic engineering brings the possibility of profound changes in the most basic physical structure of man, his genes. My reviewers of these pages have been keen to keep me within scientific and biblical bounds, as best we can determine them reasoning together. Since almost all accomplishments in genetic engineering in humans still remain future, for once, evangelicals have a chance to formulate ethical principles "before the fact." In most other applications we have arrived extraordinarily late. Perhaps this work will be a stimulus in that direction.

Genetic engineering could be beneficial or demoniacal. Many severely debilitating medical problems have long been known to be genetic in origin. Virtual elimination of these problems is possible through genetic engineering. More direct and indirect links between genes and diseases are being found almost daily. Many think the possible elimination of disease is only limited by time and technology.

The other side of this story is potential abuse. Bizarre changes in man's physical and mental structure are suggested by some. Other changes are not so bizarre but seriously bring into question basic human values. The potential for abuse is limited only by the imagination. We will explore both sides of these possibilities.

Physiology of Genetic Engineering

The individual cell, as the most basic "unit" of biological life, performs all those functions that are characteristic of living things. Some complete organisms, such as bacteria, consist only of one cell.[198] Aggregations of specialized cells form tissues and organs. These are joined to form whole organisms, such as man. Even these complex systems are derived from one reproductive cell that receives the genes and other cellular material, with all the necessary information to construct the whole. Although every cell in any organism contains this information (see Cloning), only reproductive cells and a few exceptions in nature (for example, the onion root and the nuclei of the cells that line the intestines of frogs) have the capacity to activate this total store of information into a whole organism.

Since our concern is medical ethics, I will confine myself to genetic engineering in humans. In sexual reproduction genes from a male and female gamete (germ cell) unite to form a zygote that will grow into the adult organism. Certain plants and animals, however, do not reproduce in this manner. Thus, everything here does not apply to the entire plant and animal kingdom. The ethics of genetic engineering in plants and animals is another complex ethical subject in itself.[199]

Manipulation of genetic inheritance began in 1865 with Gregor Mendel, a monk, who noticed that certain characteristics of peas could be produced by selection of the seed-producing plants. His work remained unrecognized by the scientific community for 35 years. The framework, however, for his work had been laid by Charles Darwin's *Origin of Species* in 1859 that dealt with the variability of characteristics within species, even though Darwin had no idea how these were transmitted to subsequent generations. In 1953 Drs. J. D. Watson and F. H. C. Crick discovered the double helical structure of DNA. Later, they and others worked out the sequence of the biochemical structure that "encodes" (that is, carries the information) for its own replication and the production of other chemicals within the cell. Until these discoveries, genetic manipulation had involved only experiments on the selection of mates with desired characteristics. For example, thousands of experiments were done with the fruit fly to breed various colors, wing structures, and other variations. Some characteristics could be produced in patterns that did not even occur in nature. These "new" species were called hybrids. In agriculture, hundreds of plants have been "engineered" in this way. Examples of animal hybrids are the mule (from a horse and an ass) and "hybrid" bass.

As the genetic structure and its relationship to characteristics in the offspring became better understood, direct manipulation of the genes themselves became a theoretical possibility. Desired changes could be made more selectively and specifically.

Even though complex information is stored in genes, they are formed from a simple alphabet. The four basic chemicals ("letters") of this alphabet are adenine, guanine, thymine and cytosine (nucleic acid bases). They are designated by geneticists by their initials: A, G, T, and C. Together with other chemicals (deoxyribose and phosphate) they form the basic unit of the gene structure, the nucleotide. These units are then connected to each other by a variety of chemical bonds into long chains, some with thousands of sequences, called chromosomes. All the chromosomes are then contained within the nucleus of the cell. The aggregate complexity of the chromosomes is awesome. A single strand of DNA inside a human cell contains the information of one billion bits of computer memory (500 pages of double-spaced typewritten pages).[200] The translation of this information into technical language written in English would require 1000 volumes of fine print, single-spaced (if we understood all that it says).[201] The DNA found in the chromosomes of a single human cell, that itself measures only a few thousandths of an inch in diameter, when stretched end-to-end and not in its coiled structure, would extend over a yard in length![202]

When a sperm enters an egg, each contributes one-half of its chromosome. The zygote, then, is formed with paired chromosomes from each parent and contains all the information needed to produce the physical characteristics of the future adult.

The first divisions of the zygote produce individual cells, blastomeres. These cells have unique characteristics:[203]

1. One or more blastomeres can be removed from the aggregates, and the remainder can produce a whole organism.

2. Individual blastomeres can develop into a whole organism.

3. Cellular aggregates derived from two or more zygotes and combined into one larger mass, can develop into one organism. Even aggregates of different species may combine to develop into one organism.

These studies have not been confirmed in man, but identical human twins become separate individuals well after the first division of the zygote. This event is evidence that the same characteristics of blastomeres are true in man. After the eight-celled stage the cells of the embryo begin to differentiate and lose their capability to produce a whole organism. (Non-identical or fraternal twins are caused by the fertilization of two eggs by different sperm.)

These characteristics of the blastomeres are evidence that other parts of the nucleus, as well as the chromosomes, carry instructions for the development of the organism. This transfer of additional information is rarely discussed in relation to genetic engineering, but it exerts considerable influence on cellular characteristics. (In the next chapter we will discuss this non-nuclear mechanism at some length to explore the limits of our knowledge of man's composition.)

Since the nucleotides form specific sequences, certain chemicals (restriction endonucleases) can be used to break their long chains at precise locations. Then, the severed DNA can be "recombined" with the DNA sequence that contains the desired changes. Thus, recombinant DNA (rDNA) is the name given this procedure. The newest and most promising technology in this area is the use of viruses (more accurately, "retroviruses") to direct this substitution of DNA sequences.[204] In this way the desired instructions can be written directly into the nucleus of the cell.

Retroviruses have been used to "design" bacteria to produce human insulin and growth hormone, substances that had been costly to produce and then only in small amounts. Retroviruses have also been used to "engineer" a type of bacteria that is designed to "eat" (more accurately, to digest into harmless chemicals) oil slicks that occur from tanker spills. Thus genetic engineering does not pertain to humans alone but has a wide variety of actual, as well as potential, uses.

Changes in multi-celled organisms may be made in three ways. First, non-germ (somatic) cells may be "engineered" without affecting the remainder of the organism. For example, a defect in diabetes (mellitus) is a failure of the pancreas to produce enough insulin to metabolize glucose within the body. With recombinant DNA (theoretically; it has not yet been done) the pancreatic cells could be altered to correct this defect without affecting the cells of other organs. Second, the DNA of the zygote could be altered and, since all cells are derived from this one cell, all cells of the body would have this change. For example, a propensity to one type of diabetes (mellitus) is inherited through the chromosomes of the parents. If this defect were corrected in the zygote, then neither the person nor his offspring would develop diabetes. Third, genetic changes could be made in the sperm or eggs of the adults (germ line) so that their children would have normal genes. This procedure is called "negative" eugenics because the defect would eventually be eliminated from the human race. With this inheritable type of diabetes, the parent's (only one might be affected) or parents' germ cells could be changed so that their child would have the normal genes to produce insulin. Each method raises its own ethical issues.

Defining an Ethical Approach

Dr. French Anderson, Chief of Laboratory of Molecular Hematology of the National Heart, Lung, and Blood Institute, approaches the ethics of human gene therapy according to four levels: 1) somatic cell therapy that corrects a genetic defect in the body's cells, 2) germ line therapy that corrects the defect in the reproductive cells of one or both parents, 3) enhancement therapy that would augment a normal characteristic, such as additional growth hormone to develop a taller and more muscular person, 4) eugenic therapy that would improve complex human characteristics, such as personality, intelligence, character, and the formation of body organs.[205]

These distinctions are made on the basis of current and future development of technology from the simplest (correction of somatic cells) to the most complex (eugenics). The categories are useful because changes in somatic cells only affect the one individual, but changes in germ line cells will affect all subsequent offspring. Enhancement and eugenics, however, are artificially separated because both involve a change in the offspring supposedly for the better. It is impossible to separate changes in a body from the person who occupies it! For example, a child engineered to make extra growth hormone to become a super-athlete may not like sports and decides to become an artist instead.

A distinction between monogenic and polygenic traits must also be made. Monogenic traits are those determined primarily (or entirely) by one site on one chromosome. Polygenic traits are those determined by more than one site (and possibly on more than one chromosome). Most traits that have actually been identified (that is, those that have been "mapped") are monogenic. Much less is known about the specific sites of polygenic traits. Obviously, polygenic traits would be considerably more difficult to correct. Thus, it would seem that there should be considerable success with the correction of monogenic traits before the correction of polygenic traits is attempted.

The most important categories for ethical discussion are the correction of a clearly defined disease or defect (gene surgery) and the "improvement" of "normal" physical or mental characteristics of a person (eugenics) regardless of whether they involve somatic or germ cells. These categories may in some cases be difficult to separate. For example, an offspring expected to be quite short might be programmed to increase his production of growth hormone. The extra height, however, is not necessary for that person to achieve those successes that are most important for life: his vocation and his relationships to God, to his family and to others in society).

Assumptions of Genetic Engineering

Many scientists who advocate and do research in genetic engineering make certain assumptions that may not be readily apparent. First, they assume that man is an evolved animal who is composed only of biochemicals. That is, man has no component other than his body. But the Bible teaches that man has a soul or spirit, as well as a physical body.[206] Moreover, he is made in the image of God who is pure Spirit without a body. Thus, the erroneous assumption of scientists who disregard biblical data is that all man's problems are physical; they ignore the moral/spiritual. Carried to its logical extreme, they must assume that there is virtually no problem that mankind faces that could not be addressed by genetic engineering!

Second, abortion is likely to be a routine part of the protocol for genetic engineering. We have seen how abortion is already routine in many reproductive procedures. In fact, this "escape valve" is probably one reason that scientists are not more worried about "monsters" that might be produced through mistakes. Aberrations could simply be aborted and the process repeated until successful.

The technology for genetic screening is already possible. By amniocentesis a needle is inserted into the amniotic sac (the bag of waters that an unborn baby lives in) and cells removed from the fluid for examination. By chorionic villous sampling a piece of the placenta (the organ that connects the baby to its mother and allows nutrients to pass through to it, called the afterbirth) can be removed for examination.

Third, the embryo is not considered to be a person according to commonly accepted criteria for "personhood." Thus, experimentation on the embryo is possible *with no expectation that it will be allowed to grow beyond the time that it is used for experimentation.* "Psychic (meaning certain brain functions) personhood is a rationally defensible boundary for invasive research involving human embryos and fetuses."[207] This assumption is a vital part of planned research because the necessary information for genetic engineering will be learned only by experimentation on embryos. Currently, experimentation is limited to the first two weeks of embryonic development, but who will monitor experimentors to see that this period is not extended? Who can guarantee that it will not be extended beyond two weeks when more knowledge is "needed?" It seems, then, that "personhood" is more a term of convenience for researchers than an identity that will guarantee protection under state or federal laws!

State of the Art: Moral and Experimental

The state of the art is best presented according to Dr. Anderson's categories. Possibly, by the time that this book is published, the first human experiments on somatic cells will have taken place.[208] As currently planned, these experiments are conservative and within moral bounds. They involve the extraction of bone marrow from severely debilitated patients with neurological problems, the insertion of the correct gene sequence in vitro, and the re-insertion of the marrow cells back into the patient.[209] These patients are so severely debilitated that it would be difficult to make conditions worse. The worst result would be death, although that is not likely. If these experiments are successful, then the door would be opened to correct other genetic defects in a similar manner. All future work has been prohibited until these initial attempts have been successful (see following).

In Anderson's second category " . . . gene therapy of germ line cells, would require a major advance in our present state of knowledge."[210]   His conditions are interesting and pertinent.[211] 1) "There should be considerable previous experience with somatic cell gene therapy that clearly establishes the effectiveness and safety of treatment of somatic cells." 2) "There should be adequate animal studies that establish the reproducibility, reliability, and safety of germ line therapy . . . 3) *There should be public awareness and approval of the procedure . . . .*" Currently, his conditions are reflected in the proposed guidelines of the National Institutes of Health. That is, "The Recombinant Advisory Committee will not at present entertain proposals for germ line alterations . . ."[212]

In his third category Dr. Anderson states, "Except under specific circumstances . . . genetic engineering should not be used for enhancement purposes."[213] These circumstances do not include engineering to satisfy "personal desires," such as increased growth hormone to make larger athletes for sports, but only for the purpose of "preventive medicine." For example, blood cholesterol could be lowered in otherwise "normal" individuals. The water muddies at this point, because the modern medical ethic is so materialistic in its orientation. Since every person has several such "problems," this exception could be "the thin edge of the wedge" to allow for reasons that are only eugenic.

Finally, the science for eugenic alterations simply does not now exist. Many years will be required to develop the techniques to produce such changes.[214] Dr. Anderson does not think that we should "meddle in areas where we are so ignorant."[215] I agree. We may, however, see that others are not so reluctant.

The Image of God and "Kinds"

"And God created man in his own image, in the image of God He created him; male and female He created them (Genesis 1:27).

Timothy was an FLK ("funny looking kid"[216]) in the newborn nursery. He had three extra digits, a cleft palate, and a family history of retardation with early death. Eventually, he was diagnosed to have Trisomy 13.[217] By three years of age Timothy had been seen by numerous specialists in three cities and had had surgery for his cleft palate. Throughout his life he cried almost constantly. His parents had financial difficulties because of his medical bills and the extra time that they found necessary to give to him. The stress that his condition placed upon the family is evident in the fact that his mother became depressed and attempted suicide shortly after he was born. Both parents are Christians. They have one older, unaffected child.

Such children are cited as reasons for the mindset that would declare only those who are (more or less) without obvious defects to be persons. My contention, however, is that even someone like Timothy is no less created in the image of God and has the right to all the moral, legal and social considerations of any human being.

At first glance the image of God in man would seem to have little relevance to a discussion of genetic engineering. Admittedly, its application is somewhat circuitous. It is important, however, to establish that man is a unique creation. That he is "one of a kind" is a fact that must be valued highly and he must be treated in a manner consistent with the place that God has given him. There are scientists who suggest applications for genetic engineering that violate this position and their suggestions should therefore be prohibited.

Conservative Christians (at least those who are biblically consistent) believe that individual human life begins at conception.

That is, a person is formed when an egg and a sperm unite.[218] Biblically, three exceptions to this definition would have to be made. Adam and Eve were not the result of the union of a sperm and egg (Gen. 2:7, 21-25) and neither was Jesus Christ (Mt. 1:18-25; Lk. 1:26-38). Another definition excluding these exceptions, is that human beings are Adam and all his descendants.

Still another unique characteristic that may be used to define human beings is their creation in the image of God (Gen.1:26-27). As we will see, this image is present in the fertilized egg, the embryo and the fetus. What constitutes the image is not entirely agreed upon by our best theologians, but there is considerable agreement in certain areas.

Because a discussion on the image of God can be complex, I will begin with four assumptions that should help us to simplify those matters that concern us here. (Those who would want to pursue the full argument should consult my references.[219]) 1) The image of God is still present in man after the sin of Adam and Eve, even though it is markedly distorted. 2) "Likeness" and "image" are synonyms, even though some Christians have tried to show that these words have different meanings. 3) Man is dichotomous, that is, he has two components, a body and a soul. I am quite familiar with the trichotomous view of body, soul, and spirit but I am convinced of the dichotomous view from an extensive review of the subject. Within this view, soul and spirit refer the same non-material component according to its relationship to the body.[220] 4) The Reformed view of the image of God is most biblical, differing substantially from the Roman Catholic, Lutheran, and Arminian views.[221]

The image of God consists of man's righteousness, his mind (intellect and will), his assigned dominion over the animals and the earth, his "in-created" (Kuyper's term) knowledge, and possibly, his ability to communicate and have fellowship with others and with God. There is room for disagreement here, but these characteristics seem to be those that are unique for man in comparison with the remainder of God's creations.

Man's body is generally considered not to be that image because God is totally spirit without physical form or substance. Dr. John Murray clarifies this perspective when he says that *so far as the soul is united to the body*, the body can be considered to be one dimension of the image of God. Thus, the position of some pro-life Christians that forty-six chromosomes define a human is wrong. Some animals have forty-six chromosomes and some humans have more, or less than, forty-six.[222] The true pro-life position, instead, is that human life depends upon the presence of the soul from the time of conception.[223]

When Adam and Eve sinned, they lost the perfect righteousness (sinlessness) which God had initially endowed to the human race. In His marvelous grace, however, He sent His Son as a sacrifice that we may be "re-created" into that righteousness. Christians are familiar with this re-creation or being "born-again." (The most accurate term is regeneration.) Few, however, may be aware that this re-creation may take place even before birth and, presumably, at conception as well.[224] Dr. Kuyper goes into some detail in his argument that regeneration may occur prior to birth. We should not be too surprised at this. Many Christians believe that their children who die before birth are nevertheless saved. Kuyper argues that if regeneration is a prerequisite for salvation, then these unborn children must be regenerated. Another argument comes from the biblical examples of God's work in individuals prior to their birth (Lk. 1:44; Jer. 1:5).

Dominion is one aspect of the image of God, even though unregenerate man, as he goes about his tasks, is no longer conscious of subservience to His creator and to His laws. This assignment, however, pertains to the adult more than to the unborn child, so we need not discuss it further here.

Our main focus is the image of God as it is reflected in the mind and "in-created" knowledge. My five theologians of reference (Louis Berkhof, Abraham Kuyper, John Murray, John Calvin, and Gordon Clark) agree that these characteristics are functions of the soul or spirit. Since we have established that unborn children have a soul, then we would expect them to have at least some evidence of mind and knowledge. My task here, then, is to demonstrate that unborn children have this aspect of the image of God. My evidence is from the Bible and then from observed studies of the characteristics of the newborn.

From the Bible we have the example where John the Baptist "leaped for joy" within his mother's womb at the arrival of Jesus who was also within His mother's womb (Lk. 1:44). At this moment John was six months post-conception. For Bible-believers this passage clearly communicates a reasoning process. Somehow, John knew that Jesus had appeared and he responded to the presence of his Lord with a leap of joy.

Jeremiah is another example:

> Before I formed you in the womb I knew you,
> And before you were born I consecrated you;
> I have appointed you a prophet to the nations (Jeremiah 1:5).

At first what God is doing may not be apparent. Notice that he is "programming" Jeremiah to become the person that He has planned for him to be. To be able to understand and proclaim God's Word, the prophet must have certain intellectual abilities. Fashioning of Jeremiah in this way is at least part of what this passage means. It is God's "in-created" knowledge (see above) of Jeremiah to perform the tasks that God has planned for him. As an unborn child, he could not have been developed in this way without the presence of his mind.

From observed studies we have examples that the newborn already "knows" a great deal.[225] As early as 42 minutes, a baby may be able to distinguish between vision and muscular action. At two weeks, an infant knows to avoid an object that is going to hit him. As a child learns to communicate, he distinguishes those sounds that convey language, (the human voice) from those that do not, (the sounds of a refrigerator). Further, there is considerable evidence that the ability to learn language is an inborn, not learned ability.[226]

We also have evidence from studies of unborn children. Brain activity, an indirect measurement of mental activity, can be measured electrically (by an EEG or electroencephalogram) as early as 45 days. They can squint, swallow, and move the tongue by 9-10 weeks. By 12-13 weeks they can suck the thumb and recoil from pain. (They can even try to escape from pain as gruesomely displayed in "The Silent Scream.") While these activities are little more than animal instinct, they are the early parameters of the future minds of persons.

Another characteristic of the image of God, not discussed by the theologians cited, is communication or fellowship. Communication is an important dynamic among the Persons of the Trinity, first in eternity and then in time, when the Son was Incarnate. The Lord's Supper is also known as Communion (a communication between God and man). The Greek word, koinonia, used to designate this sacrament, is also used to designate fellowship among believers, demonstrating the similar nature of the two activities.

Communication (as fellowship) involving the verbal dimension distinguishes man from the animals. They are not able to communicate to the degree that man may communicate with others and with God. This process depends upon the message sent from a rational mind to its reception in the rational mind of another in the form of a rational communication. That communication can occur in children and adults is easily understood, but its application in the embryo, fetus and infant seems to be limited, if it can be applied at all. Thus, we would have to conclude that the image of God in these stages would be their *potential* to develop rational thought and communication.

Thus, the image of God as a profile of characteristics unique to man establishes that he is "one of a kind." As such, he cannot be mixed with other "kinds." He is the whole entity that comes into existence with the union of a sperm and egg. He is composed of a physical (body) and non-physical (soul or spirit) regardless of the presence of defects or their severity (man's greatest defect is spiritual, caused by Adam's disobedience).

The argument sometimes put forward that the conceptus, the embryo and the fetus, does not have a soul is specious. To select any time other than conception for the entrance of the soul is completely arbitrary because there are no parameters by which the presence of the soul can be detected.[227] The same problem exists at the other end of life if one seeks to define death as the time that the soul departs the body.[228]

As "one of a kind," man is not to be combined with other "kinds." God created every kind to procreate after its own kind (Gen. 1:11, 12, 21, 24, 25) and He specifically prohibits the mixing of kinds (Lev. 19:19, Dt. 22:9).

The problem arises with the fact that a satisfactory classification of "kinds" has not been developed.[229] The most universal classification, as defined by Linnaeus, classifies all living things by kingdom, phylum, class, order, family, genus, species, and variety. This system, however, does not correspond to the biblical categories of "kinds" (e.g. Gen. 6:19-20; Lev. 11:1-47).[230] It has also been found to be inadequate apart from biblical considerations.[231] Thus, God's prohibition against the mixing of "kinds" has some practical limit to its application. Still, Christians' approval of genetic "cross-breeding" and the development of hybrids must not be automatic. That He has established some limits is clear.[232]

One modification of this principle should be made. God's prohibition on the whole does not apply to its parts. On this basis genetic sequences could be taken from animals and inserted into human genes *as parts, rather than wholes.* Many gene sequences in animals are identical in their structure and function to those in humans. If either were examined apart from the whole genetic structure *in vivo,* no differences could be detected. Thus, parts are distinct from the identity of the whole because the whole would differ at many sites.[233] This failure to distinguish between the characteristics of a whole and its individual parts is called the Fallacy of Division, an informal fallacy in logic.[234]

Thus, the substitution of a normal gene sequence from an animal for the abnormal gene sequence in a human would not be the mixing of kinds – as transplantation of organs is not a mixing of kinds. Brain transplantation may be an exception because the brain (physical) has a unique and intimate relationship to the mind (spirit).[235] The union of a sperm (or egg) from a human with the egg (or sperm) from an animal, however, *for whatever reason,* is biblically prohibited because each represents a "whole" of its kind.

The use of retroviruses as agents to splice genes would not seem to violate this mixing of kinds, either. We have seen that viruses are probably a unit of life, as unicellular plants and animals are. Thus, their incorporation into human genes is not a mixing of wholes but the addition of a part (the virus) to a whole (the DNA).

Clearly, man is unique among all other living things because he is descended from Adam and is created in the image of God, and therefore, a "kind." Union with any other living "kind" would be a violation of God's natural law that creatures procreate after their "kind."

Eugenics

The term "eugenics" dates back to 1883 when it was applied to the hope that the human race could be improved by allowing the brighter and more productive members to have children and by restricting the "misfits" from having any children at all. As we have seen (Chapter 1), many laws were passed (that remain on the books today) in the attempt to carry out the restrictive aspect. These "designers of the human race" had to become more subtle in their approach after Hitler's program of undisguised eugenics.[236] Today, the phrase "quality of life" is substituted for "eugenics" and genetic engineering has become the vehicle by which this improvement of the human race is to take place. It promises such planners greater and more specific design than earlier advocates could have dreamed. We must not let them blind us to the past. It is possible that the atrocities of the past could pale before those of the future, all in the name of "improving the human race."

There are two basic questions to consider concerning eugenics. What is the biblical morality of the process itself and what is the motive of those who advocate it?

Programming Morality. The morality of eugenics is determined by the characteristics that are sought in the offspring. The most desirable goal for those who advocate changes seems to be an increase in intelligence. Dr. Joseph Fletcher has said that, " . . . quality control in birth technology should select for intelligence, on the ground that control is human and rational, and is therefore, to be espoused."[237] Most notorious is the sperm bank that carries only the sperm of geniuses and Nobel Prize winners. Of course, that bank is concerned with intact sperm rather than the genetic manipulation of the sperm or egg, but the intent is the same.

The moral issue is whether greater intelligence *per se* will benefit the human race. Certainly, greater intelligence will produce greater technology. The problem, however, is how to use that technology. Alfred Nobel invented dynamite to move through earth and rocks much faster than men and machines previously could. Immediately, however, dynamite was used in bombs to destroy other men and their property. Greater morality is the greatest need for mankind; not greater technology. The morality of the users, not intelligence, determines the great usefulness or destructiveness of technology.

For example, we can look at the "intelligence" of two Nobel prize winners. In 1974 Sir Francis Crick worked out the double-helix arrangement of DNA. His plans included that " . . . no newborn infant should be declared human until it has passed certain tests regarding its genetic endowment . . . and if it fails these tests, it forfeits the right to live."[238] Linus Pauling, a Nobel Prize Winner, has suggested that every young person have a tattoo on his forehead that represents his genotype:

> "If this were done, two young people carrying the same seriously defective gene in single dose would recognize the situation at first sight, and would refrain from falling in love with one another."

Such extreme views clearly reveal that greater intelligence does not automatically produce better morality. The very people whose work makes genetic engineering possible cast serious doubts about whether it should be done. Their plans do not include much personal freedom. So much for the advantage of intelligence!

Such grandiose plans should not blind Christians to the plans that God has to improve the human race. That plan is found in the Great Commission. The highest goal to which man may be conformed is the image of Jesus Christ (Rom. 8:29; II Cor. 3:18). And, God has determined how this transformation is to take place (John 3:1-8; Rom. 12:2; II Cor. 5:17). Further, His people are to develop the fruit of the Spirit (Gal. 5:22-23), righteousness (Mt. 6:33), and gifts of the Spirit (I Cor. 12:1-11). This program definitely does not include genetic engineering! Such spiritually determined effects cannot be produced by physical (biochemical) means.

Other changes include the elimination of all genetic causes of disease, more proficient athletes and manual workers, and various changes of character and personality. These designs are similar to those that are proposed for clones (which see).

The Motive. Advocates of plans to further eugenics through population and birth control and artificial insemination have shown that they will use any means to achieve their ends. Theirs is *an attempt of a few to gain power over all.* They have the mindset that "superior" persons should control others. The issue is the same as any other proposal that sets criteria for what is "good" (moral) and what is "bad" (immoral). Who decides?

Dr. Francis Schaeffer simplified the issue. He observed that such decisions can be made in one of four ways: by one person (in effect, a dictator), an elite group (who may be scientists or others of "special" intelligence), a majority of people (ruled out by the methodology itself), or biblical revelation.[239]

The central issue must be clear: *Whenever anyone speaks of what is good or bad for an individual or society, regardless of the means, the moral values of the decision-makers will inevitably be imposed on the non-decision makers.* For example, those scientists who subscribe to Humanist Manifestos I and II, if given the opportunity, would gladly attempt to program Christianity out of existence because they clearly state that Christianity is not "good" for the human race.

Goals of the eugenics movement cannot be accomplished without complete control over the sexual and procreative methods of *everyone.*[240] Any omissions would allow the continued propagation of the very characteristics that the planners are attempting to eliminate. That is a power that no state has had in the history of the world. As the eradication of smallpox required a global effort, the eradication of "bad" genes would also. The ultimacy of this power is illustrated by a parody of God's creation of man: "Let us make man in our image." With genetic engineering, as with eugenics of the past and social programs of the present, some men desire to make all men in *their* own image. The contrast is striking: in creation man is made in the image of the perfect God; but scientific design is to make all men in the image of a sin-infested and sin-infected humanity!

To a great extent Christians and non-Christians alike associate technology and science, particularly in health and medical issues, with a general intention to do "good." The non-Christian, and even the professing Christian, however, cannot determine the good apart from a thorough knowledge of biblical revelation. Motives can be misguided by biblical ignorance: "There is a way which seems right to a man, but its end is the way of death" (Prov. 14:12). C.S. Lewis has provided prophetic insight into the motives and behavior of scientists in two books, one fiction, *That Hideous Strength* and the other non-fiction, *The Abolition of Man*. We ignore his warnings to our peril.

Another presumption that may not be explicit, is clearly implicit in genetic engineering – the perfectibility of man.[241] Since earliest times philosophers and others have proposed means to obtain some kind of utopia. The Christian knows this dream is impossible because mankind remains under the curse of the sin of Adam and Eve and the ongoing maladies produced by personal sins. This orientation to sin cannot be eradicated from the human race. Utopia for the Christian is heaven. This presently unreachable goal, however, does not preclude an increasing reformation of society through the Great Commission and an increasing obedience to the Word of God. Utopia for the unbeliever will never be realized.

This idea of perfectibility obscures the fact that we are already "fearfully and wonderfully made" (Ps. 139:14) and only "a little lower than God" (Ps. 8:5a). Further obscured is the reality that, without scientifically engineered physical changes, the Christian is being made into the image of Jesus Christ (II Cor. 3:18). So, biblically a balance must be maintained between the sinfulness that will always characterize humans individually and socially, the high status of man as he is created by God, the present transformation that is taking place within believers, and the future "utopia" that is our hope.

Another major fallacy of eugenics is its hypothetical product. "Improvement of the human race" has little to do with individuals. The individual is sacrificed for the whole. Individual freedoms are given up entirely. If one is fortunate, he may not be one of the sacrificial victims. Even so, the entire control of his own destiny has been taken out of his hands should he have "bad" genes.[242]

Central to a biblical/medical ethic is a conscious recognition and practical outworking of the "darkness" of man's mind and intentions without regeneration and revelation. Two manifestations of this darkness are a quest for power over other men and the dream of a utopia in which peace and happiness exist for all. *Eugenics is not a scientific but a religious issue, totally wedded to one's anthropology.* What man *is* determines how, and to what extent, he can be manipulated.

CHAPTER 6

As interns, we had a busy obstetrical service. In a twenty-four hour period it was not unusual to deliver twelve to fifteen babies. Since the patients were almost entirely wives of young military men, most deliveries were uneventful and routine. From that experience, however, two deliveries stand out in my memory. First, a set of twins had complications during labor on Christmas Day, 1969, and one died. With twins, complications are common and expected (although rarely does death occur). The second delivery began routinely. As the head extruded with the face down (the most common presentation), I routinely used a bulb syringe to remove mucous and amniotic fluid from the baby's mouth so that this material would not be inhaled when he gasped and cried to begin breathing. When I placed my finger in his mouth (which I could not see because of his face down position), the delivery stopped being routine. Where the upper lip was supposed to be, two deep crevices were felt that extended far back into the mouth. After the entire body was out and he could be turned over, I could tell that he had a complete, bilateral cleft lip and palate. All I could think about was breaking the news to the mother and the number of surgeries that would be required to give some normality to his appearance and function.

Genetic Repair: Present and Future Dangers

The correction of genetic defects (genetic surgery) at both the somatic and germ cell levels is the extension of medical practice to the deepest level of the physical structure of the human being. For example, phenylketonuria (PKU) is now treated with a special diet but in the future the genetic defect that causes the enzyme deficiency might be corrected.   This gene surgery would be considerably more effective since it would be a one-time instead of a lifetime treatment.   The ethical problems involved in this procedure are 1) its potential unintended effects and 2) the determination of what is a defect.

Paul Ramsey has raised serious questions about the dangers of genetic repair.   He proposes to allow only the correction of defects that have no cure or relief of symptoms and those that are devastating.[243]   For example, he would favor genetic repair of Tay-Sachs disease, but not cystic fibrosis because some medical "relief" for this problem is already available.   The correction of diabetes would be "immoral."   More details of his positions are provided in his book.   The following will be a review of those issues in which genetic repair faces the same ethical considerations as other practices in medicine.   Then, we will review issues that are unique to genetic repair.

First, the use of science to justify power over other people has been presented under Eugenics.   Conclusions then should be transposed here where they apply.

Second, the potential effect on future generations is an area that has not been given adequate ethical consideration.   The effect of diethylstilbesterol on the daughters of women who took it during their pregnancy is one example.[244]   Worldwide, people take enormous amounts of medication that have the potential for untoward effects, including alterations of their genes.   While genetic engineering may have more potential to affect future generations, the problem is already with us and is inadequately addressed.

Third, the movement from animal experiments to humans is an unavoidable sequence in the development of new treatments. If current research and its transfer to humans is ethical, then a proscription against genetic repair on this basis is invalid.

Fourth, harmful effects are a potential consequence of every type of treatment. The efficacy of a treatment should always be weighed against its beneficial effects. Again, medical ethicists give too little attention to this area, especially since benefits of many (if not most) medical treatments are overvalued while their unintended effects are underestimated.[245]

Fifth, the greatest difficulty is to draw the line between what is and is not a defect. Even here, however, the problem is not new. Current medical practice considers wrinkles, excess fat, sagging cheeks and hips, large noses, and small breasts to be defects that can be corrected by plastic surgery. The ethics of such procedures have not (to my knowledge) been addressed from a biblical perspective, so we will briefly review the subject here.

The Bible does not place great value on one's physical appearance, as God strengthens a person through his "defects" (I Sam. 15: God looks on the heart; Is. 53: Christ's figure was not appealing, II Cor. 12: Paul's weakness and appearance were not attractive). I am not saying that cleft palates, esophageal atresias, severe burns, skeletal contractures, and other anatomical defects that cause disease and life-threatening disability should not be corrected. Plastic surgery solely to enhance appearance, however, would seem to have little biblical support.

Initial work in gene surgery will not grapple with this issue because all current proposals call for the correction of defects that are severely debilitating and mean a shortened life span. It is a "nothing could be worse" situation that is in view. If these attempts are successful, however, the issue of enhancement will be upon us in full force.

No definition of "defect" will be adequate to cover all potential abuses of genetic engineering, but one that is carefully constructed may have some protective value. Eventually each defect must have ethical review because of the many possible varieties.

I will attempt some moral definition of what is and is not a defect. Surely, further modification will be necessary when and if these procedures become a reality. Always, we must attempt to derive such principles from the Bible as consistently and thoroughly as possible. A) The defect must have a genetic etiology, one that has been located at a specific site(s) on the human chromosome. The correction of a defect that is caused by more than one defective gene (polygenic) should be preceded by considerable experience and success with defects that are caused by a single gene (monogenic). B) The problem to be corrected must be clearly a medical disease or deformity that would otherwise require chronic medication or treatment. C) The potential benefit must clearly outweigh any potential harmful effects. D) The disorder must cause death prior to a "normal" life span according to both biblical and natural occurrence.[246] E) The disorder causes physical pain. Psychic pain would not qualify because its criteria would be too vague to be practical. F) The disorder must prevent the fulfillment of God's directives. Examples include the ability to work at some useful task (Eph. 4:28; I Thess. 4:11), to contribute to the body of Christ (I Cor. 12), to have children (see Chapter 1), to support one's family (I Tim. 5:8), and to have sexual intercourse with one's spouse (I Cor. 7:1-5). G) These criteria cannot override other biblical principles. For example, one should not steal in order to pay for the expense of genetic repair (which is likely to be considerable).

These criteria restrict the use of genetic repair. We should not fool ourselves that, just as with plastic surgery, what is done has a great deal to do with the moral values and subjective interpretation of the predominant medical or cultural worldview. We have seen Dr. Anderson's category of enhancement of "normal" characteristics. Elsewhere, I have discussed the relativity of "normality"[247] and Dr. Ramsey has accurately assessed how "repair" blurs into "enhancement." Unless medical ethics takes a more conservative direction, abuse of genetic engineering will surely occur. This abuse may be no worse, however, than some current medical abuses, such as abortion. The development of new technology should not be prevented because of its potential for abuse. If so, we would have to eliminate every procedure (medical and otherwise) that we currently do, because a negative side to every one exists![248]

Seventh, the insertion of the correct gene affects the total person. That is, genetic insertion may correct the defect but cause some other adverse condition because the whole is affected by the sum of its parts. Currently, this point is only conjecture but who knows what interaction among genes may occur when a substitute replaces a gene to which the whole organism has already adjusted?

Eighth, grotesque human deformities may be produced. Again, this problem has occurred in medical practice. The most familiar examples are probably thalidomide babies. With genetic engineering, as in nature, severe genetic abnormalities are likely to be incompatible with life. Thus, the "monsters" of science fiction are mostly just that – fiction. Still, if genetically treated babies did occur, our standards against abortion and infanticide would still prohibit their destruction: all the more reason to be quite certain of what we are doing.

Cloning

Cloning is the reproduction of organisms with identical genes. Identical twins or triplets (or more!) in humans is an example of cloning that occurs naturally.[249] Since every cell in a human body contains all the genes of the individual, each cell has the information to produce another identical body. As cells differentiate into specialized tissues and organs, they lose potential to produce all the other parts of the body, but a mechanism might be found to restore this ability and to produce clones (whole organisms).

Another possible method to make clones would be to extract the nucleus from the cell of an adult and insert it into an enucleated egg that has been found to have the capacity to grow into a whole organism. Another method is to tap the potential in each embryonic cell (up to the eight-cell stage) to develop into a complete individual, each with the same genes. One of these cells could be divided at the eight-cell stage, separated again, and the whole process repeated *ad infinitum*. Dr. Duane Gish discusses actual attempts at cloning (that have not been successful) and the inherent dangers in the process, including the ridiculous claim by David Rorvik that a human being has been cloned from a dead man.[250]

At first glance cloning attractively offers a solution to many common problems.[251] For example, individuals of great achievement in business, art, science, law, and other disciplines could be duplicated, thus offering more of their "greatness" to the world. Scientific studies in humans could be simplified because the control of most variable factors that are crucial to scientific endeavors could be eliminated. Selection of desirable characteristics in children by potential parents would be possible. Incompatibility in organ transplantation would be eliminated because the genetic structure of a donor and recipient could be identical. Teams of people, such as astronauts, might work together more efficiently with less friction in close environments.

These answers, however, are not as simple as they first appear.[252] Parents and teachers of identical twins know how different they can be and how they have conflicts with each other, as non-identical brothers and sisters do. Before and after birth their exposure to physical and psychological stimuli varies. Motivation and discipline are also variables in a person's development and achievement.

It is really impossible for two people to be raised entirely alike. Clones would have their particular affect on each other, as identical twins and triplets do. In his unique book Dr. George E. Vaillant describes how people change markedly over a lifetime, some even to the extent that their whole orientation to life is different.[253]

The greatest change that can occur in a person is regeneration and sanctification. By God's power that person, an enemy of God (and therefore an enemy to others and to himself), becomes a child of God whose thinking and behavior begin to be conformed to the image of Jesus Christ. Peter is one graphic example of this transformation. Thus, the person from whom genes are taken at one point in his life may become quite a different person later because of this re-birth. Who could tell which clones God might pick for Himself?

Other serious limitations of cloning on the scientific level could be described, but they do not seem necessary because the immorality of cloning is clear. The argument is similar (that is, a cloned argument!) to that against eugenics. Who determines value, that is, the characteristics of the person to be cloned? Value is a moral (spiritual) concept that has nothing to do with physical attributes. Further, great power must be granted to those who (think that they) know these values in order to manipulate others according to their designs. A limited number of clones would not be possible; these planners would have to be sure that an entirely "balanced" world was programmed. Accidents or failures to plan would be inexcusable according to their design.

Suppose a clone decided to be a carpenter rather than the super-athlete that he was programmed to be? What would be done with him? With the difficulties that young people have choosing careers and the dissatisfaction with one's work that abounds, our world has a wonderful balance that some have called a "division of labor." In the traditional concept of vocation ("calling") God endows each person with characteristics that differ sufficiently to carry out His creation mandates. Surely no man (or men) has the ability to plan vocations for the entire world! Only God can do that. Science fails often in its prophetic role with nuclear energy, population control, public education, and welfare. How dare it attempt to master the hopes and dreams of the entire human race?

The world-wide existence of abortion makes cloning seem ludicrous. The fifty million "workers" aborted each year could surely supply whatever additional skills and services the world needs, given a free society in which they may pursue their "callings."

The Interface of Genetics and the Spiritual Realm

Most, and perhaps all, variations in physical characteristics (phenotypes) can be explained on the basis of current knowledge about genetics. Still, we cannot ignore the biblical fact that man has both a body and a soul from the moment of conception.[254] In fact, pro-life Christians fail to establish an adequate basis for individual human life beginning at conception unless they include the argument for the presence of the soul.[255] Eve was not created in the sense that Adam was. In fact, God has not created anything since the first week of Creation except for the Incarnation of Jesus Christ and the regeneration of believers (II Cor. 5:17).[256] Thus, the physical characteristics of all subsequent people were present in Adam's chromosomes.

Certain characteristics are difficult to explain unless one postulates God's active intervention in the genetic process. Perhaps the most difficult to explain is racial distinctions. We have a clear account of the origin of languages and the impetus for migration of peoples all over the earth (Gen. 11:1-9). Were there racial distinctions prior to that time or did God acti-vate/de-activate certain genes when He caused changes in their language? We do not know because God has not revealed it. We must not, however, back off from such difficulties. We must strive to harmonize science with Scripture, being careful always to give the priority to Scripture. Concerning the origin of racial distinctions Dr. Arthur Custance has given one explanation on the basis of known genetic variations.[257]

That God does actively intervene in genetic inheritance seems to have happened when Jacob bred Laban's flocks (Gen. 30:31-43). Jacob knew that

> even in a flock of solid-colored animals there would be some that were what modern geneticists called "heterozygous" – that is, they had within their genetic endowment the ability to produce a small proportion of off-colored progeny. Many, of course, were "homozygous" and when two homozygous animals mated, they could produce only the dominant coloration in their offspring.[258]

By random selection many more solid-colored progeny than off-colored should result. In this case, however, many more of the off-colored were born.

> Though Jacob could not know which of the goats and sheep were heterozygous, God knew, and He saw to it that only these mated with the homozygous animals (or with each other) so that a much greater proportion than normal turned out to be ring-streaked, spotted, and speckled. God later revealed to Jacob in a dream that this is exactly what had happened (Gen. 31:10-12).

Modern humanists base all inheritable characteristics on genetic influence because they believe that *physical* reality is the *only* reality. Christians, however, should consider it possible to attribute some characteristics to the spiritual component of man. There are only two options: either every person's spirit is identical and only the physical component is different (including the genes) or both the physical component and the spirit are different. It does not seem tenable to believe that God used but one mold for our spiritual side while making all differences physical.

If our spirits differ, then at least some human characteristics must be attributable to the influence of that spiritual component. As genetic research continues, we must be careful to remember that each person is affected by his spirit, as well as his genes, even though the separation of the influence of each may not be clear. For example, the differences in identical twins is not necessarily due to the slight variation in their genes. It may also be due to qualities in their spirits. Thus, in twins separated at birth, all differences cannot be be attributed solely to their different environments, as is usually concluded.

God is continuously active in His universe: " . . . for in Him (God) we live and move, and have our being . . ." (Acts 17:28a, KJV). " . . . in Him (Christ) all things hold together" (Col. 1:17b). " . . . He (Christ) upholds all things by the word of His power" (Heb. 1:3b). Theologically, this activity is called God's Preservation.[259] By inclusion, His continuing activity must be present in genetic processes as well.

Dr. Lawrence Dillon, a genetic scientist, seems to have more insight than most. He sees the necessity to account for an ordering mechanism for the complex events that occur within cells.[260] Many who are knowledgeable of the microscopic functions of the cell know that all cellular processes cannot be explained on the basis of genetic coding alone. Something instructs the genes themselves when to "turn on and off." Like a light switch, they cannot do it themselves. Dr. Dillon has called this ordering mechanism, the "Supramolecular Genetic Mechanism." (This mechanism also has been called "dauermodification."[261]) Many genetic scientists do not agree with Dillon's analysis, but the complexity of cellular processes and the Doctrine of Preservation demands some explanation of this activity within cells.

It would be an overstatement to say that the Supramolecular Genetic Mechanism is God's Preservation within cells. It would be accurate, however, to say that no matter what becomes known in the future, it will always be necessary to reckon with God's ordering of His Creation. To say that we will eventually have all the answers to all these unknown mechanisms, is to ignore the results of scientific investigations. "New" knowledge always ends with more questions than it answers, a trend characteristic of scientific investigation since it began. There is no reason to believe that we will now begin to answer more questions without simultaneously increasing the number of questions.

Some Christians have taken the position, as scientific knowledge has advanced, that God accounts for the "gaps" in that knowledge. As this knowledge has increased, God has been relegated to smaller and smaller "gaps." The true biblical position is that God preserves His creation and explains the "why" of *all* phenomena. For example, why do two bodies in the universe attract each other? To say that their attraction is inherent in matter is to describe, not to explain, it. The Christian rules out chance when he says that, at creation, God declared that such an attraction should exist. Further, God is continuously active in His universe. The argument, here, is biblical and logical (neither is inconsistent with the other when both are understood and applied properly[262]). The biblical evidence has already been presented.

The logical argument lies between the Deist and Theist positions. Deists hold that God created the universe, set it in motion, and now passively refuses to intervene in any way. Orthodox Christians have never considered Deism valid. Theism is based upon the above truths, logical conclusions of many verses, *and* miracles such as the crossing of the Red Sea and the "signs and wonders" of the Incarnate Jesus Christ that have occurred when God has intervened in the course of history. Further, if God is omnipotent, then He cannot "give up" His power at any time. That is to say, any "effect," no matter how indirect or secondary, has its ultimate "cause" in God Himself. Otherwise, He would be conditioned by that very power that He had given up and would at that point be less than omnipotent! While my comments about this topic have been brief, you will find that Dr. Henry Morris has discussed the relationship between the power (energy) in the universe and God's power.[263]

If God is everywhere actively present, then He is also active in the processes of all living things. One manifestation of His presence is in animals and in man as soul or spirit (different words for the same entity[264]). Of course, a qualitative difference exists between the soul/spirit of animals and that in man because man is made in the image of God and descended from Adam (see previous chapter). This difference is particularly applicable to God's preservation in genetic engineering.

The ultimate question in genetic engineering is, "Can a man be constructed entirely (both cytoplasm and chromosomes) from simple biochemicals?" If he could, would he have a soul?[265] One eminent Christian scientist, Dr. A. E. Wilder-Smith, believes that this "creation" would have a soul.[266] It would seem however, that his conclusion is highly unlikely because the cellular processes are far more complex than have been thought. Indeed, *I contend that such a construction of either plant, animal, or man from biochemicals alone is impossible.*

Scientists have long recognized that living things have a unique quality, lacking in inorganic matter. Creation scientists (Christians who do not believe that some evolutionary process must account for "scientific" evidence of long periods of time, such as fossils and radioactive dating), like scientists before the theory of evolution was postulated, believe that this unique characteristic is sufficient to say that life cannot arise *spontaneously* from non-life.[267] I carry their principle one step further: animal and human life cannot be constructed from simple biochemicals alone. *Thus, the design of man can be generated only by God's special creation, natural procreation from other life, or the manipulation of the nucleus and cytoplasm of living cells that already exist.* The presence of life must have a quality imparted to it that only God can give. For animals and man that explanation would seem to be the soul/spirit.

For plants that quality is not clear. Still, as Dillon has postulated, something must control and coordinate the complex processes even within plant cells. These complex actions seem to preclude the mere assembling of these biochemicals together. Morris postulates that plants are not alive in the "biblical sense."[268] His argument is based upon the "silence" of Scripture. That is, the Bible makes no explicit statement that plants have a soul, as it does concerning men and animals. Such arguments from silence are speculative. Even if plants do not have a soul in the biblical sense, they still possess some quality that is not present in inorganic materials and that was specially created "in the beginning."[269] Any assembly of plants by man that had the same biochemical structure as a living cell would still lack the quality that carries on its functional processes.

The next problem is how this "life controlling function" becomes present in offspring. In man this concept is the heart of the traducianism vs. creationism debate. *Creationism* here refers to the theological position that the soul of each person is specially created by an act of God at the moment of conception and must be distinguished from the creationism that is concerned with origins (cosmology). *Traducianism* is the position that the soul is propagated from the parents. It is my belief that traducianism is by far the stronger of the two positions.[270] There are several reasons, but I mention only two. First, creationism requires that God create a *sinful* soul. Orthodox Christians teach that man's guilt is two-fold: federally in Adam as he represented the human race and, personally within himself, as a sinful disposition leading to sinful acts. Second, God completed His work in six days and rested on the seventh (Gen. 2:2; Ex. 20:11). That is, He stopped creating. (Jesus Christ's body was specially created at His incarnation, but His Incarnation was unique in history.[271])

The current understanding of biological inheritance favors traducianism. All the characteristics of the offspring are transmitted from the parents either through cellular components (DNA and structures in the cytoplasm). If, as we have proposed, the infused quality that gives life to non-living matter is spirit (soul) in animals and man, then this quality would also be transferred to the offspring. In humans this quality could include a regenerate or an unregenerate soul. Traducianism is more consistent with the whole process.

As should be apparent, these arguments are not "essentials" of the faith. Perhaps creationists and traducianists will never convince each other. Further, Dr. A. E. Wilder-Smith may be right that such a unity has been created by God between a particular arrangement of basic biochemicals and an associated life "energy," that upon the creation of the former, the creation of the latter is inevitable.

These are questions for serious debate. Anyone who says that science will or will not achieve a goal had better be prepared to be proven wrong. Sometimes science requires a re-thinking of biblical interpretations as the challenge to the Copernican theory did. While science is not a source of truth found in the Bible, it may expose conclusions wrongly derived therefrom. Most likely, we will have to wait many years for science to identify all the building blocks of life forms (if it ever does), and in particular, those in man. But the question of how to treat these "created" beings ought to be addressed *beforehand* by our best theologians and laymen to help determine whether our reasoning here is consistent with the most tenable biblical position.

CHAPTER 7

THE ETHICS OF LIFE AND DEATH

Evangelicals are familiar with Christ's promise "that (we) might have life, and have it abundantly" (John 10:10b). We associate that promise with the peace, hope, and joy that comes from our reconciliation to God and our obedience to His commandments. Perhaps we are not as familiar with the concept in the first part of that same verse, "The thief comes to steal and destroy," the opposite to Jesus' work. The false messiah causes discord, despair, and emptiness. Both the positive and the negative sides of this verse are usually associated with *spiritual* consequences for the believer or the unbeliever. This verse and others, have a clear application to the health of the *physical body*. We will explore that application as a foundational principle for Christian health professionals, that is, a biblical/medical ethic. The practice of medicine is secondary to a concept of health, as health is determined by a concept of life and death.

The Bible places all issues into two categories that are described as light and darkness, truth and error, good and evil, righteousness and lawlessness, and life and death. Our concern is with life and death. Three texts serve to illustrate this contrast. 1) Through Moses God spoke to the Israelites: "See, I have set before you today life and prosperity, and death and adversity . . . So choose life in order that you may live, you and your descendants" (Dt. 30:15, 19b). 2) Man at his best still fails: "There is a

way which seems right to a man, but its end is the way of death"
(Prov. 14:12). 3) "Now He is not the God of the dead, but of the
living; for all live to Him" (Lk. 20:38).

The dominant worldview within modern medicine ignores God,
and is even anti-God. As such, it is death-oriented. Therefore,
its fruits have become, in particular instances, the intended death
of patients (e.g. abortion and euthanasia). To ignore and despise
God will inevitably cause death in one of its forms.

The Bible recognizes only two systems. One is associated with
God and life. The other is without God and associated with
death. If a Christian does not understand this fundamental incompatibility of the current philosophy within medicine and
biblical life, then he can never make the distinctions necessary to
a biblical practice of medicine. By consequence, he cannot provide
the most complete approach to health for his patients, and worse,
may impart death when he intended life.

What Are Life and Death?

"Life" and "death" are used as though they were simple concepts. They are, however, much more complex than is readily
apparent. In our approach we will move from the biological to the
biblical in order to contrast the ordinary understanding of life and
death with a biblical understanding. The Bible, not common or
cultural opinion, must be our ultimate source of definitions.

Most simply, life is the absence of death. But, what is it that
characterizes an "alive" organism? First, it assimilates material
from its environment into itself. Second, this material is used to
produce energy and to replace used materials. Third, a period of
time exists when this assimilation results in growth in size and
complexity. Fourth, this assimilation results in the production of
energy. Fifth, waste products must be eliminated. Sixth, disease
or injury must be overcome or healed. Seventh, reproduction must

occur or the life of the specie will cease with the present generation. Eighth, the organism reacts to external stimuli.

As I state these criteria, I realize that these characteristics are not present in all living organisms throughout their lifespans. Growth and reproduction are present only at certain periods. The other six characteristics, however, must always be present. When any one or more of these processes ceases, death occurs.

Biblical concepts markedly change these characteristics. First, the spiritual dimension of reality is introduced in addition to the physical. Second, a Living Being (God) is described Who is entirely Spirit and who is entirely sufficient within Himself. For Him none of these characteristics of biological life apply. Third, there are other spiritual beings who have none of these characteristics of life. They are of two kinds: good (those who serve God) and evil (those who serve Satan). Fourth, man is composed of a spiritual (non-physical) element as well as the physical.

Fifth, there are four environments where life is determined by the obedience of men and women to certain conditions set forth by this All-sufficient Being. The first environment was a Paradise where man was placed with the condition that he not eat of the tree of knowledge of good and evil (Gen. 2:16-17). After his disobedience, his environment changed as he was discharged from Paradise and placed under a personal curse (Gen. 3:14-16) and an environmental curse (Rom. 8:19-22; I Cor. 15:42-58). Therefore, man has an opportunity to be changed through regeneration, the beginning of the reversal of the personal curse. Finally, two future environments exist as the destiny of men, eternal peace and joy or eternal discord and despair, depending upon the presence or absence of regeneration in each person.[272]

In essence *life is communion with God*. Basically, this communion has two aspects – knowledge and obedience:

> If we say that we have fellowship with Him and yet walk in the darkness, we lie and do not practice the truth; but if we walk in the light as He Himself is in the light, we have fellowship with one

another, and the blood of Jesus His Son cleanses us from all sin
(I John 1:6,7).

Obviously, one must "know" where to walk and then must obey in
order to have fellowship with both God and other men (the same
Greek word in the New Testament, *koinonia*, is translated both
communion and fellowship). Right knowledge and right action
are *ethical* concepts. Thus, biblical life is an ethical concept.

A biblical definition of death will correspond to a biblical
definition of life. It can be derived from the types of death that
are described in the Bible. There are four. (Some applications of
these states to euthanasia have been made elsewhere.[273]) One is
biological death (Mt. 9:18; I Cor. 15:3, 12-19; I Thess. 5:16b). A
second is the second death (Rev. 2:11; 20:6, 14; 21:8). This state
is the final judgment of Jesus Christ of the unregenerate. A third
is the person who dies to his former self and way of life as a
result of regeneration (Rom. 6:2-14). The fourth is God's curse
on Adam and Eve after their disobedience in the Garden of Eden
(Gen. 2:15-17), under which the unregenerate continue as long as
they remain outside of Christ (Rom. 7:24; I Cor. 15:22; Eph. 2:1,
5). Thus, with the exception of the Christian's death to his former
way of life, death is a consequence of sin.

Death, biblically understood, is a *spiritual change or separation
of one's relationship to God, to other people, to oneself, and to one's
residence.* This change may be for the better or for the worse.
The central concept here concerns one's relationship to God in
obedience or disobedience. This relationship is ethical, having to
do with right and wrong, righteousness and sin. The wrong
orientation to God causes a wrong orientation to oneself and to
others contrary to what God intended originally in the unity of the
human race.

One might wonder why unregenerate men do not fear separation from God since this state is the fullest realization of death.
First, they *do* fear death. Scripture speaks of those who "through

fear of death were subject to slavery all their lives" (Heb. 2:15). They "suppress the truth" (Rom. 1:18) and, therefore, this fear is neither conscious in their minds nor in their communication to others. Dr. Rousas Rushdoony is likely correct in his assessment of this suppression of fear:

> because the sinner is in revolt against God, he does not experience the fear of death as fear of separation from God, but rather as a fear of separation from life.[274]

Thus, he is willing to sacrifice everything to prevent his own death. An example is the common expression, "Better red than dead," meaning that it is better to yield to Communism than to fight and die for the cause of freedom.

Man's disorientation apart from God is apparent. On the one hand, he wants life at all costs. On the other hand, he often seeks death as a solution to the problems of life. These biblical concepts of life and death compel Christians to apply them in medical situations. The critical factor is the addition of *ethical criteria that are established by God and that affect both man and his environment.* This factor is not substantial (physical or material), but entirely spiritual. A definition of life becomes dependent upon this ethical relationship. *Therefore, medicine as the discipline that maintains and assists in the restoration of human lives must define what enhances and what destroys life according to this ethical relationship.*

Health, righteousness, and life are closely related concepts, as are sickness, sin, and death. They are not identical because the spiritual takes priority over and at times may supersede physical health. For example, the missionary does not choose the most physically healthy situation for himself and his family by going to some remote region. He is, however, doing that which is most spiritually healthy, because his going results in a more complete communion with God than if he did not go (assuming that he is indeed called to the mission field). Most graphically, martyrs give up physical life entirely for their spiritual health.

Separation from Communion (Communication) with God

Christianity is the only religion[275] that consistently and in every way promotes life. This reality is seen in the transformation of the Western world where biblical values came to predominate. Thus, once backward and barbaric nations have freedoms that are unparalleled in human history. With that transformation came unprecedented health. Scholars may debate whether there is direct cause and effect here, but the fact that the spread of Christianity and these developments were simultaneous is undeniable. By contrast, what have other religions produced?

In India where Hinduism is dominant, widespread poverty continues. Alongside of malnourished children lacking protein in their diets are cattle that could supply this protein were it not for the religious taboo against eating their meat. Although actual death is not always the immediate consequence, death is present in the retardation of physical and intellectual growth. The poverty of the people in general (*infra*) is a consequence that closely approximates death. Without sanitation, proper nutrition, and immunization, the death rate, especially for the younger ages, is much higher than in Western countries.

The Muslim religion claims hundreds of millions of followers worldwide. One distinctive of its teaching is fatalism. Whatever happens is "Allah's will." On the surface, this teaching appears somewhat similar to Calvinism which recognizes that all things are directed by God's will. However, Calvinism has a strong emphasis on personal and social responsibility. One cannot make the excuse that "God willed it" when a result could have been avoided by following biblical teaching. That Islam stifles personal and social responsibility to prevent and treat disease and death is apparent.

Secular humanism is without question a religion. Even the Supreme Court has ruled that it is, and Humanist Manifestos I and II clearly present humanism as a religion. Thus, the various aspects of death that are called for in these documents is consistent with their approach to life that excludes, and is even hostile to God. "Freedom" for women to have abortions and for all to have "death with dignity" are examples. There is even an organization called, "The Society for the Right to Die." Its nonsensical name is apparent. All men die regardless of rights! This title is consistent with man's only choice other than God and the life associated with Him.

As Western man has lost his identity with God, he has also lost his place as the most valuable living organism. Protection for all non-human forms of life is actively sought simultaneously with the death of unborn children by the millions. Death for the physically defective and the elderly receives active lobbying in the legislatures of our land. Elevation of animal life over human life is strangely twisted thinking, but is a consistent application of a philosophy that excludes God.

The epitome of man's attempt to separate himself from God and the resulting association with death is found in the Enlightenment influence that caused the French Revolution. The movement was consciously a revolt against any supreme, supernatural authority that dared to tell man how he should live. The result of that attempt has become known as the Reign of Terror. Man's fear is most fully realized when he is most consistently aligned against biblical revelation. Death and destruction are the inevitable result.

We must never lose sight of the fact that ultimately there are only two religions: the one defined by the supernatural revelation of God's Word (best described as Christian theism,[276] and the defined without that revelation (the broad category of naturalism). These have been discussed in some detail previously.[277] Further,

Dr. Gary North has extensively demonstrated the similarities of demonism and the occult with humanism.[278]

Separation from One's Creator: Self-Destruction

In medicine a common belief is the association of poverty with an increased incidence and prevalence of disease and death. This belief is only partly true because poverty primarily consists of the ethics of a group, rather than the presence or absence of wealth *per se*. Of five factors responsible for famine, only weather is a factor beyond man's control.[279]

The "Protestant work ethic" has been much maligned, but it is a major factor in overcoming the problem of poverty. Certainly, it can be carried to the extreme where responsibilities other than one's employment are neglected. Short of that extreme, the productive nature of that ethic should be fully appreciated. First, diligence of labor will produce an abundance of food or the money to purchase it. Second, the certainty that the universe is an orderly, predictable system because its Creator and Sustainer has made it so, has resulted in a science that has been able to understand something of the spread of disease so that it can be controlled by appropriate sanitation and immunization. Again, the development of this science in the West where Christianity prevails is an association that should not be ignored.

Wealth alone does not produce maximum health. Literally, men and women are killing themselves in the midst of wealth. In the United States there are clearly avoidable causes of disease and death. Lung cancer caused by cigarette smoke is the second leading cause of death in the United States and accounts for one-third of all cancer deaths each year. Cirrhosis of the liver is the third leading cause of death, frequently caused by alcoholism (there are common causes other than this for which a person is not morally responsible). If one surveys the other eight leading causes of death, he will find other avoidable risk factors, such as stress, alcohol, and poor nutrition (the ones already named), and too much food and too little of the right kinds.[280]

The lives of some of the world's wealthiest men provide graphic examples of the dissociation of the individual possession of wealth and disease and death. For example, we can review the ends of the lives of nine of the world's richest men in 1923. One died in bankruptcy after living his latter days on borrowed money. One died penniless in a foreign country where he had fled to escape justice. Another died abroad insolvent. Another died insane. Two spent time in prison. Finally, three died by suicide.[281]

This "self-destructiveness" clearly reveals that man is death-oriented apart from God. In the United States both the knowledge and the means are available for greater physical health, yet the major killers are "self-indulgence." Without an ethical re-orientation man can do little to combat his downhill course.

One foundational principle for a biblical worldview in medicine, then, is *that obedience to God's law and principles produces health and life.* The disease and death associated with poverty are overcome by regeneration and re-orientation to God's word causing a person to become responsible and thus more productive.[282] On the other hand, *re-distribution of wealth in the form of medical care to the poor will not (and has not) overcome their disease.* Wealth without orientation to God still produces disease and death. A biblical view of poverty and wealth as it relates to health and disease calls for *repentance of both the wealthy and the poor.* Health is not available any other way.

At first glance, Sweden and Japan may seem to contradict this dissociation of wealth and a biblical worldview. A closer look, however, minimizes this impression. First, both Japan and Sweden have both had strong Christian influences at some time in their history. Second, both are building upon the bodies of aborted babies. Third, Sweden's suicide rate is high, parental authority (e.g. spanking) has been severely eroded (see next section), and they depend on others for national defense.

Separation from Others: The Family

The family, as the basic unit of society, is a life- and health-promoting institution. When no one else cares, the family is concerned for its own. Even those who are "evil" give good gifts to their children (Mt. 7:9-11). In our society, however, an anti-family bias is clearly present. The violation of the integrity of the family is directly a cause of disease, and not infrequently, an actual cause of death.

Abortion not only causes the death of a potential new addition to the family, but complications for the mother that may include sterility, bleeding, perforation of the womb, infection or "psychological" problems. Millions both fear and experience various forms of sexually transmitted diseases (STD) each year;[283] these are entirely avoidable and could be eradicated almost entirely within one generation simply by obedience to God's design for sex expression and intimacy only within marriage.

As all birth control methods have side effects, the avoidance of pregnancy has many complications. The intra-uterine device (IUD) may perforate the womb or cause serious bleeding and infections. (It is also an abortifacient.) The birth control pill (oral contraception) may cause heart attacks, strokes, blood clots that can damage the lungs, and other side effects that may require medical attention (see Chapter 2).

This anti-family bias is seen in the present health emphases of state and federal governments. Billions are spent to prevent or treat the problem of smoking, alcohol, and drug addiction. At the same time the government supports immoral sexual practices through its provision of birth control measures (including abortion) and the "non-judgmental" treatment of STDs. In any state minor girls can be treated for these problems without parental consent or notification. A double attack on the family exists here. First, the promotion of immoral sexuality is destructive to the commitment necessary to maintain an intact family. Second, that these "medical" practices can be performed without the parents' consent undermines parental authority and cohesiveness.

It is well-known among family physicians and is documented with research that families with interpersonal conflicts and divorce have more real and imagined medical problems than stable families. When these interpersonal conflicts are successfully managed through counseling, visits to the doctor's office are markedly reduced. Further, there is extensive documentation that the health and longevity of married men and women is much greater than those who are single, regardless of age.[284]

God's emphasis on the importance of the family unit is seen in His death penalty for sexual immorality in the Mosaic Law.[285] At first glance His punishment seems harsh, but the necessity of the family for a healthy society justifies this penalty, if only at a human level. (On a cosmic level God's laws are just – simply because *He* makes them.) If the sanctity of life requires the death penalty when innocent life is taken, then the direct threat to life that results from the violation of the sanctity of the family necessarily requires a similar penalty.

Death as a "Solution"

Today, there seems to be an increasing number of instances in which individuals and cultures propose and practice the death of other human beings as a solution to their problems. Such a solution is the clearest illustration of the result of a worldview that is not ethically oriented to God's revelation.

Materialism, the excessive desire for material possessions, causes death in ways that directly concern the medical profession. In more than ninety-five percent of abortions, the decision is clearly made on the basis of convenience. The pregnancy interferes with the plans and desires of the woman, so her solution is to choose death for the unborn child. Evolution, as one example of a worldview that ignores God, provides a justification for these choices since man is but another animal. Even abortion for the so-called hard cases, rape, incest, and a severely deformed fetus (2-5 percent of pregnancies), is a choice of death over economic, social, and "psychological" cost.

Euthanasia[286] is similarly a solution for a variety of reasons. The problem may be the day-to-day hardship of caring for someone who is severely or chronically ill, a desire to have immediate access to an inheritance, or as a solution to the escalating costs of care for the elderly. Infanticide involves similar choices at the other end of the life spectrum.

Suicide may be interpreted as the ultimate in self-absorption[287] because death is seen as the answer to one's problems. No one else is considered except as the distorted intention of the suicidal person to free others of the burden that he perceives himself to be to them. Materialism, as a response to the loss or indebtedness of large sums of money, is frequently a factor here also. Murder may be a less common, but nevertheless, frequent answer to interpersonal problems. The seemingly simple solution is to get rid of the other person rather than spend the time, effort, and physical resources to sort out and remedy problems.

Utilitarianism is a dominant philosophy in modern medicine denoted by such terms as "quality of life" and "the good of society." In perhaps the most advanced application of medical practice, eugenics by genetic engineering, death is inherently part of the protocol. First, there seems to be little moral reservation to experiment upon human embryos and then simply flush them down the sink. Second, if mistakes are made, they can similarly be handled, or if the mistake is recognized after implantation into a woman, it can be aborted.

In some political systems the answer is to kill one's opponent(s) or put them in prison (a form of death). The present government is seen to be ineffective and hopeless, so that a severe corrective action must be taken. That physicians sometimes participate in these regimes demonstrates the link of medical practice to one's politics.[288]

The Sixth Commandment stands as a bulwark against these "solutions." Consistent non-Christians, as one told me personally, see no distinction between allowing a disease to progress naturally to end in death and giving an injection to end the life of a suffering patient. God has not intended killing others as a solution. He has given us all the biblical means with which to solve problems in every area without this option. *The Christian can assume that any decision that calls for such death of another person or persons as a solution to a problem situation is in antithesis to the revealed will of God.* If we ever contemplate the death of a person or persons as a solution, it should be a red flag of warning that we have not chosen God's way.

The Bible, however, seems to allow certain exceptions: just war, self-defense, and capital punishment.[289] Actually, killing in such situations is based upon such an elevated view of the sanctity of life that *those who directly threaten or destroy* the life of others must forfeit their own lives. "Whoever sheds man's blood, by man his blood shall be shed, for in the image of God He made man" (Gen. 9:6). Thus, *as a last resort in those situations where life has already been taken or is immediately threatened* death is prescribed. It should be noted that even here, however, death is not seen as a solution but an act of punishment.[290]

Finally, in situations with terminally ill patients where the better course is not to prolong death, death is not a solution, but an inevitable consequence of the disease process. Death is allowed because man is limited in his efforts to prevent death.

Ethics of Life: Reversal of the Death Process

Two basics are absent in a non-Christian worldview: the need for regeneration and a willingness to improve one's own situation and the situation of others. Regeneration (often called "the new birth"), however, is widely misunderstood among Christians. Either term is biblically accurate, but the words "born-again" are too loosely applied by both Christians and non-Christians. The change of which the Bible speaks is dramatic: "transformation" (Rom. 12:2, II Cor. 3:18), "a change of mind" (II Cor. 7:10), "made alive" (Eph. 2:5), "a new creature" (II Cor. 5:17), and "renewal" (Rom. 12:2, II Cor. 4:16, Tit. 3:5). The state of a person changes from darkness and death (Eph. 2:1) to light and life (II Cor. 3:18).

The entire physical universe is under the sentence of death, having been "subjected to futility" and "corruption" (Rom. 8:19-22). This sentence of death is clearly seen in the Second Law of Thermodynamics that states, "an orderly system always proceeds toward disorder without an input of additional usable energy." "Nature" left to itself can only cause death and destruction as an ultimate end. Correspondingly, the universe will be regenerated when Christ finally comes to reign (Mt. 19:28). It is fascinating that the only times the Greek word for regeneration, *palingenesis*, is used in the New Testament are: once concerning man (Titus 3:5) and once concerning the physical universe (Mt. 19:28). Other words (as noted above) are used to convey the characteristics of the new birth, but the actual word, regeneration, is only used in these two places.

The definitive character of this change must be realized. It is an ethical re-orientation.[291] Whatever source of ethics one has followed until this point is renounced for God's Word as the basis of one's ethics. Simply, it is a re-orientation from self-centered-ness to God-centeredness. This re-orientation amounts to obedi-ence to the Ten Commandments. We have seen several examples where they apply directly to issues of life and death and therefore health and disease.

What conclusions can we draw for the practice of medicine from a biblical concept of life and death?[292] 1) Christians who work in medicine and medical ethics must increasingly become conscious that only two worldviews exist: that governed by God's supernatural revelation and that governed by man within himself. It is obvious that humanism, as a medical philosophy, has resulted in many practices that are contrary to the biblical worldview.

2) Life, health and righteousness are the opposites of death, disease, and sin. All diseases and death result indirectly from the sinful state into which Adam and Eve plunged the human race, directly as the result of personal sin or as a part of God's sovereign plan (Job 2:1-6; John 9:1-3). The ultimate death is final separation from God. "Death with dignity" is opposite to the biblical concept of death. The choice of God's way is not only a choice leading toward spiritual life, but usually toward physical health and life as well. Much, if not most, diseases are avoidable by this "way." God's promises are mostly spiritual, but they have real physical impact. Perfect health is reserved for heaven, but a maximal degree of health is possible by ethical re-orientation. We who practice medicine are obligated to make this identification. A violation of God's moral law has severe consequences in a similar way that a violation of natural laws does. For example, the violation of the law of gravity will result in a fall that causes injury or death.

3) A corollary is that medical practice is first and foremost dependent upon a biblical ethic. The Ten Commandments, as they are meant to reflect considerable breadth, summarize a great deal of this necessary ethical re-orientation.[293]

4) A great deal of the medical care and cost in the United States is directly related to sin. Modern medicine supports the sins of people by its "non-judgmental" approach.

5) Sanctity of life involves the whole of the biblical ethic. The pro-life movement has become so closely identified with the sanctity of physical life that in some instances it ignores other important values. Perhaps the most apparent is the oversight, and sometimes refusal, to face financial limitations in the provision of medical care. To ignore this wider application and identify this sanctity with only abortion, infanticide, and euthanasia is to restrict

its biblical application. Further, spiritual values take precedence over physical health. For example, the missionary who threatens the health of himself and his family when he goes to "regions beyond," believes (rightly) that his proclamation of the gospel takes precedence over that concern.

Other specifics may be found throughout this book. My intent is to help all Christians know what is darkness and what is light within the practice of medicine.

> For he who finds me finds life,
> And obtains favor from the Lord.
> But he who sins against me injures himself;
> All those who hate him love death (Prov. 8:35-36).

NOTES

1. Tierney, *"Fanisi's Choice,"* 26. In an about–face from previous positions that generally opposed "pro-life" positions, *Science* magazine presented an excellent article that pointed out many fallacies of the population planners.
2. Aristotle, *Politics*, 327.
3. Thielicke, *Theological Ethics: Sex*, 215.
4. Tierney, *"Fanisi's Choice,"* 32.
5. Norman, *"Will World Population Double?"*
6. Clark, *"Population and Land Use"*. (page number not given)
7. Muggeridge, *"The Overpopulation Myth,"* 117.
8. Chilton, *"Planned Famine,"* 1.
9. Carlson, *"Famine 1985."* All the information in this paragraph comes from this reference or Note 8.
10. Finkelstein, *"Hard Work."*
11. Norman, *"Will World."*
12. Kuehnelt-Leddihn, *"Some Reflections,"* 77.
13. *Ibid.*, 74.
14. Scorer, *Life in Our Hands*, 96.
15. On an average 2.4 abortions must be done to prevent one live birth because the woman will be returned to the fertile state sooner than if she had completed the nine months of pregnancy. She will also not experience the relative infertility produced by breast feeding (see Chapter 2). Experience in several nations is consistent with this fact. Further, it is likely that the widespread availability of abortion reduces the effective practice of contraception because contraception is no longer the "last hope" to prevent the birth of an "accidental" pregnancy. (Potter, *"Additional Births,"* and Brackett, *"Effects of Legalizing Abortion."*)
16. Kuehnelt-Leddihn, *"Some Reflections,"* 72.
17. *Ibid.*, 74.
18. *Ibid.*, 71-72.
19. *Ibid.*, 78.
20. Kazun, *"The Population."*
21. Thielicke, *Theological Ethics: Sex*, 217.
22. Young, *"Literature, Literacy,"* 50-51.
23. Dyck, *On Human Care*, 48.
24. Carlson, *"The Malthusian Budget,"* 43-46.
25. Simon, *"The Rhetoric of Population."*
26. Carlson, *"Famine 1985."*
27. Murray, *Principles of Conduct*, 45-46.

28. The importance of these verses and those that Jesus had in mind touching the subject of divorce should not be underestimated. The rampant divorce among Christians has been further aggravated by misinterpretation of these and other relevant passages. The clearest and most thoroughly biblical treatment of this subject is found in Adams, *Marriage, Divorce, and Remarriage*.

29. Thielicke, *Theological Ethics: Sex*, 203.

30. Packer, *"Situations and Principles,"* 164-5. Also, see "Voluntary Childlessness" later in this chapter.

31. John Jefferson Davis, *Evangelical Ethics: Issues Facing the Church Today*, Phillipsburg, NJ: Presbyterian and Reformed Publishing Company, 1985, pp. 14-16.

32. *Ibid.*, p. 14.

33. Murray, *Principles of Conduct*, 78; Thielicke, *Theological Ethics: Sex*, 202.

34. Adams, *Marriage, Divorce, and Remarriage*, 16.

35. "Flesh" has other meanings in other Biblical contexts.

36. Adams, *Marriage, Divorce, and Remarriage*, 17.

37. Calvin, *Harmony of the Gospels*, Vol. 2, 380.

38. Thielicke, *Theological Ethics: Sex*, 205-207.

39. *Ibid.*, 203.

40. Ramsey, *Fabricated Man*, 35-36, 56-59.

41. Hook, *"Chromosomal Abnormality Rates."*

42. Unger, *"To Multiply, Increase,"* Nelson's *Expository*, 254-5.

43. Schaeffer, *The Christian Manifesto*.

44. Murray, *Principle of Conduct*, 79.

45. *"The Cost of Raising Babies,"* Perspective, 1-12.

46. Its function in the provision of health and healing has been developed in Payne, *Biblical/Medical Ethics*, 127-138.

47. Wilson, *"Mother Didn't Know,"* 31.

48. Montgomery, *"How to Decide"*, 10.

49. Payne, *Biblical/Medical Ethics*, 63-64.

50. For a description of coerced birth control, including abortion, in China, see Mosher, "Forced Abortions."

51. Schaeffer, *No Final Conflict*.

52. Even where the life of the mother is endangered, the goal is to save both lives if possible, not to assure that the unborn baby dies (often by lethal injections), as is the current practice of induced abortion.

53. Rushdoony, *Institutes of Biblical Law*, Vol. II, 203.

54. Payne, *Biblical/Medical Ethics*, 11-26.

55. Blamires, *The Christian Mind*, 70.

56. All information in this section is from Eastland, "*Who Put the Wrong.*"

57. "Wrongful life" generally refers to a lawsuit brought by a child born with birth defects (or his or her legal representative) who alleges that the physician was negligent to advise the mother of the possibility of birth defects or failed to perform the tests that would have disclosed their presence. "Wrongful birth" refers to similar conditions except that the suit is brought by the parents rather the child. "Wrongful pregnancy" or "wrongful conception" refers to a lawsuit brought by the parents of a healthy child whose pregnancy should have been prevented by a sterilization procedure or abortion.

   I am lumping these terms under "wrongful birth" to avoid too much technical jargon and, more importantly, to focus on God's Sovereignty in every birth regardless of the number or severity of defects.

58. Kinsey, *Sexual Behavior.*

59. McMillen, *None of These Diseases. First Edition*, 45-51.

60. Dillow, *Solomon on Sex.*

61. Levin, "*Sexual Pleasure;*" Philip and Lorna Sarrel. "*The Redbook Report on Sexual Relationships,*" Redbook Magazine October 1980, pp. 73-80.

62. Smith, Robert D., "*Book Review: The Act of Marriage.*"

63. Clark, *First John: A Commentary*, 69.

64. Potts, *Textbook of Contraceptive Practice.* Hatcher, *Contraceptive Technology* 1982-83. Closely followed in this section.

65. Potts, *Textbook of Contraceptive Practice*, 77.

66. *Ibid.*, 86-7.

67. Uricchio, *Natural Family Planning.*

68. Grisez, "*Life, Death and Liberty,*" 55.

69. *Ibid.*

70. Caravan, "*History Repeats Itself,*" 79.

71. Smith, Janet E., "*Abortion As a Feminist,*" 69.11

72. *Ibid.*

73. Brackett, "*Effects of Legalizing Abortion.*"

74. Campolo, *The Power Delusion*, 31.

75. Goldzieher, "*Comparative Studies ...I*", 621. Dr. Lewis Hicks, a specialist in Obstetrics and Gynecology and a reviewer of these chapters on reproductive issues, believes that the frequency of ovulation is probably zero in actual experience.

76. Some physicians say that these problems are less common and less serious than those that result from an unprevented pregnancy but this comparison is entirely false. First, pregnancy is a natural process, whereas the use of these pills is not. Second, it is not a like-kind comparison. Pregnancy is a totally different process from that which seeks to prevent its occurrence in the first place. The hidden message in such a comparison is that the prevention of a pregnancy is preferable to the pregnancy itself because it is safer. Further, such comparisons usually involve a distortion of the available data. See Marshall, *"Birth, Birth Control"* and Hilgers, *"Abortion Related Maternal Mortality."*

77. Ory, *"The Noncontraceptive Health Benefits."*

78. Payne, *Biblical/Medical Ethics*, 79-83.

79. Ramsey, *Fabricated Man*, 42.

80. Payne, *Biblical/Medical Ethics*, 105.

81. A comprehensive study of the benefits vs. harms of birth control pills needs to be made. I have made only a brief and rough comparison here. It is a study that would have to be updated periodically, also, as new information is reported.

82. Waltke, *"Old Testament Texts,"* 15.

83. For more discussion of these laws and their spiritual and physical significance, see Kaiser, *Toward Old Testament Ethics*, 198f and Payne, *Biblical/Medical Ethics*, 93.

84. Waltke, *"Old Testament Texts,"* 17-18.

85. *Ibid.*, 18.

86. Hatcher, *Contraceptive Technology* 1982-83, 5.

87. Payne, *Biblical/Medical Ethics*, 63-64, 108ff.

88. Murray, *Principles of Conduct*, 146n.

89. Symposium, *Ethics and Medicine* 1(1):4-14, 1985.

90. Potts, *Textbook of Contraceptive Practice*, 245-273.

91. Thielicke, *Theological Ethics: Sex*, 223.

92. Calvin, *Commentaries on the Last Four Books of Moses, Vol. 2*, 33-35

93. *Ibid.*, 34.

94. Rushdoony, *The Institutes of Biblical Law, Vol. 1*, 84-85.

95. Potts, *Textbook of Contraceptive Practice*, 259-261.

96. Allen, *Ethical Issues in Mental Retardation*, 25.

97. It is necessary to use a label, such as defective, to avoid a lengthy explanation in each instance. We should remain aware that defective, abnormal, and other labels are quite relative and could apply to any one of us upon close scrutiny.

As I am using these terms, they are not meant in any way to be derogatory or indicate that any people in these categories are less than fully human or are not made in the image of God. See Payne, *Biblical/Medical Ethics*, 148-151.

98. Simon, "*The Rhetoric of Population Control*," 76.

99. *Ibid.*, 61-85.

100. Allen, *Ethical Issues in Mental Retardation*, 86-7.

101. *Ibid.*, 87-89.

102. Payne, *Biblical/Medical Ethics*, 155-180.

103. Allen, *Ethical Issues in Mental Retardation*, 19.

104. *Ibid.*, 71.

105. Reed, *Mental Retardation: A Family Study*, 39.

106. Murphy, "*Human Sexuality in the Mentally Retarded*," 614-6; Bass, *Marriage, Parenthood*, 324-6.

107. Murphy, "*Human Sexuality in the Mentally Retarded*," 624-6.

108. Ibid., 621-4; Robertson, "*Procreative Liberty*," 413.

109. Payne, *Biblical/Medical Ethics*, 57.

110. Yussman, "*Principles and Procedures.*"

111. Curie-Cohen, "*Current Practice of Artificial Insemination.*"

112. Fletcher, "*Artificial Insemination in Lesbians.*"

113. Anderson, *The Price of a Perfect Baby*, 52.

114. Payne, *Biblical/Medical Ethics*, 63-64, 108, 128-129.

115. Thielicke, *Theological Ethics: Sex*, 257.

116. *Ibid.*, 254-5.

117. *Ibid.*, 250.

118. Payne, *Biblical/Medical Ethics*, 76-79.

119. Postma, quoted in Regenmorter, *Dear God, Why*, 117.

120. Thielicke, *Theological Ethics: Sex*, 262.

121. Regenmorter, *Dear God, Why*, 121. This reference is from Dr. McIlhaney's experience. We are unaware of any studies that have been made of the family situation of AID children.

122. A traducianist must logically conclude that the sperm and egg (that eventually unite) somehow convey the soul of the parents that becomes the soul of the child. For these believers the sperm and egg would have even greater significance.

123. Wallis, "*The New Origins of Life.*"

124. Adams, *Matters of Concern.*

125. Mascola, "*Screening to Reduce Transmission.*" Also, "*Screening for Artificial Insemination Found Lacking*," American Medical News, 21.

126. *Ibid.*, pp. 1354 and 1357 respectively.

127. Curie-Cohen, *"Current Practice,"* 589.

128. Anderson, *The Price of a Perfect Baby*, 50.

129. Kristoff, *"Parents of 'Nobel Sperm' Baby."*

130. Kaiser, *Toward Old Testament Ethics*, 93ff. Murray, *Principles of Conduct*, 49ff.

131. Curie-Cohen, *"Current Practice,"* 587, 589 respectively.

132. Thielicke, *Theological Ethics: Sex*, 265.

133. Davis, *Evangelical Ethics*, 68-69.

134. "Insemination Policy Includes Singles."

135. Davis, *Evangelical Ethics*, 69.

136. "Father's Identity: The Right to Know."

137. Regenmorter, *Dear God, Why Can't We Have a Baby?.*

138. Thielicke, *Theological Ethics: Sex*, 266.

139. Payne, *Biblical/Medical Ethics*, 188-191.

140. Anderson, *Issues of Life and Death*, 49-5.

141. Collins, *"Treatment-Independent Pregnancy."*

142. Polansky, *"Do the Results."*

143. Dunn, *"Semen Examination."*

144. Payne, *Biblical/Medical Ethics*, 33-50.

145. *Ibid.*, 224.

146. Cohen, *Hard Choices*, 69-94. The original account covered twenty-five pages, so this short version is selective. The names are not real, but are the same as those that the author used. Readers are encouraged to read the original account to see the difficulties that this couple encountered.

147. The terms "in vitro fertilization" and "embryo transfer," IVF-ET or "embryo replacement," IVF-ER are sometimes used. We will use the simple designation IVF.

148. Technically, "abortion" may mean that the loss of the unborn child was spontaneous or induced. Today, abortion almost always designates an induced loss, but one should be aware that it may correctly be used to apply to a spontaneous miscarriage.

149. Seibel, Machelle M. "In Vitro Fertilization, Gamete Intrafallopian Transfer, and Donated Gametes and Embryos". *The New England Journal of Medicine* 318:828-834, 1988.

150. Walters, *"Editor's Introduction,"* 209.

151. Wallis, *"The New Origins of Life."*

152. Shaw, *"Handling of Embryos."*

153. *Ibid*

154. Wallis, *"The New Origins of Life."*

155. Bronson, *"Current Limitations."*

156. Gold, *"The Baby Makers."*

157. Ramsey, *"On In Vitro Fertilization."*

158. Extensive animal experiments do not guarantee that unexpected problems will not occur in humans, but experimentation in animals before man is a standard prerequisite for new medical practices.

159. Quoted in Ramsey, *"On In Vitro Fertilization."*

160. *Ibid.*

161. *Ibid.*, 25. Paul Ramsey speculates why Dr. Edwards may have changed his mind.

162. The falsification of data by some scientists (many of whom are quite famous) both past and present, has been well-documented in Broad, W. and N. Wade., *Betrayers of the Truth: Fraud and Deceit in the Halls of Science*, New York: Simon and Schuster, 1982. Other characteristics of unrestrained scientists are described in books by C.S. Lewis: *The Abolition of Man*, New York: MacMillan Publishing Co., Inc., 1947, and *That Hideous Strength*, New York: Macmillan Publishing Co., Inc., 1965.

163. Payne, *Biblical/Medical Ethics*, 144-151.

164. Wilcox, Allen J., Clarice R. Weinberg, John F. O'Connor, et al. "Incidence of Early Loss of Pregnancy." *The New England Journal of Medicine* 319:189-194, 1988.

165. Some Christians using *in vitro* fertilization and have adopted these restrictions.

166. Schlesselman, *"How Does One Assess."*

167. Gold, *"The Baby Makers,"* 36.

168. Tiefel, *"Human In Vitro Fertilization."*

169. Payne, *Biblical/Medical Ethics*, 119-121.

170. *Ibid.*

171. Gold, *"The Baby Makers."*

172. Nelson, *"The Ethics of In Vitro Fertilization."*

173. Steinfels, *"In Vitro Fertilization."* 11

174. Ethics Committee, *"Ethical Considerations,"* vii, 29s-31s.

175. Pritchard, Williams *Obstetrics*, 639-644.

176. Payne, *Biblical/Medical Ethics*, 59.

177. Marrs, *"In Vitro Fertilization-Embryo Replacement."*

178. Utian, "*Successful Pregnancy.*" These names are fictitional and did not appear in the original presentation of this account.

179. Rushdoony, *Institutes of Biblical Law*, 183.

180. Today, the state assumes the right to educate children, but God established it within the family. Thielicke, *Theological Ethics: Politics*, 270-288 and Rushdoony, *Institutes of Biblical Law*, 182-185.

181. Rushdoony, *Law and Society*, 171-176 (also see his other chapters on inheritance applied to other contexts).

182. Murray, *Redemption Accomplished and Applied*, 132-140, and Packer, *Knowing God*, 181-208.

183. Rushdoony, *Salvation and Godly Rule*, 275.

184. Anderson, *The Price of a Perfect Baby*, 31.

185. Timnick, "*Surrogate Money, Atonement.*"

186. Anderson, *The Price of a Perfect Baby*, 29.

187. Harlow, "*Ethology.*"

188. Payne, *Biblical/Medical Ethics*, 30.

189. Grobstein, "*The Early Development of Human Embryos,*" 234.

190. Anderson, *The Price of a Perfect Baby*, 34.

191. Kaiser, *Toward Old Testament Ethics*, 190-192.

192. *Ibid.*, 192.

193. Ramsey, "*On In Vitro Fertilization.*"

194. Tiefel, "*Human In Vitro Fertilization,*" 3237.

195. Ramsey, "*On In Vitro Fertilization,*" 31-32.

196. Nelson, "*The Ethics of In Vitro Fertilization and Embryo Transfer,*" 24-25.

197. Brungs, "*Biotechnology and the Social Order.*"

198. It is a matter of controversy as to whether viruses are "alive." From current evidence, however, they do not appear to have an identity separate from the cells that they parasitize. See Watson, *Recombinant DNA*, 14.

199. Gish, *Manipulating Life*; Anderson, *Genetic Engineering*.

200. *Sky Magazine*.

201. Wilder-Smith, "*Origin of the Genetic Code.*"

202. Stambrook, "*What the Clinician Needs to Know about DNA.*"

203. Grobstein, "*The Early Development,*" 229f.

204. *Ibid.*

205. Anderson, *Human Gene Therapy*.

206. Payne, *Biblical/Medical Ethics*, 75-79; Berkhof, *Systematic Theology*, 191-201.

207. Tauer, *"Personhood,"* 252.

208. Merz, *"Stumbling Blocks,"* 1825-32.

209. Anderson, *"Prospects for Human Gene Therapy"* and *"Human Gene Therapy."*

210. Anderson, *"Human Gene Therapy,"* 283.

211. *Ibid.*, 285-6.

212. *National Institutes of Health.*

213. Anderson, *"Human Gene Therapy,"* 287.

214. *Ibid.*, 289-90.

215. Atkinson, *"Some Theological Perspectives"*: (Part I and II).

216. FLK or "funny looking kid" is a common euphemism in medical practice. Often, the suspicion that a child has a genetic problem begins with the fact that their appearance is somehow different from that of other babies or children. It is not a derogatory term, but one used until a more definite label is diagnosed or he is proven to be genetically and physiologically normal.

217. Trisomies occur when Chromosome 13 fails to separate entirely during its phase of division. Thus, the child has part of an extra chromosome. This extra part usually does not survive to be born. When it is, a variety of abnormalities can be present. The most common trisomy is Down syndrome and involves Chromosome 21.

218. Payne, *Biblical/Medical Ethics*, 143-151.

219. Berkhof, *Systematic Theology*; Kuyper, *The Work of the Holy Spirit*; Calvin, *Institutes of the Christian Religion*; Clark, *The Biblical Doctrine of Man*; Murray, *The Christian View of Man.*

220. Payne, *Biblical/Medical Ethics*, 75-79. The same non-material entity, when viewed in conjunction with the body is called "soul"; when viewed by itself, apart from the body, is called "spirit." Although we believe that man is dichotomous, the belief that man is trichotomous would not change the following argument except to make it more complex.

221. Berkhof, *Systematic Theology*, 202-210.

222. Payne, *Biblical/Medical Ethics*, 152, note 21.

223. *Ibid.*, 144-148.

224. Kuyper, *Work of the Holy Spirit.*

225. Friedrich, *"What Do Babies Know."*

226. Custance, *"Who Taught Adam."*

227. Payne, *Biblical/Medical Ethics*, 148-9.

228. *Ibid.*, 197-211.

229. Since plants will accept grafts beyond the limits of hybridization by means of sexual propagation, biblical "kinds" may be identified with the maximum extent of sexual hybridization.

230. Morris, *The Bible and Modern Science*, 367-389.

231. Dillon, *Ultrastructure, Macromolecules, and Evolution*, 559-565.

232. Rushdoony, *Institutes of Biblical Law*, 253-262.

233. Iglesias, *"What Kind of Being."*

234. Copi, *Introduction to Logic.*

235. As we have stated in many places, man is a unity of body and spirit with their most intimate association that which exists between the brain (a part of the physical body) and the mind (a part of the non-material spirit). It is likely that the brain of an individual has some peculiar identity with the mind of that same person because of this intimacy. Although brain transplants are not now a possiblity, we ought to begin to consider the morality or immorality of such surgery. Certainly, the brain is not just another organ like the kidney or liver.

236. Gish, *Manipulating Life*, 4-5; Sobran, *"Eugenics and Euphemisms."*

237. Paraphrased in Jones, *Brave New People*, 63.

238. Quoted in Gish, *Manipulating Life*, 16.

239. Schaeffer, *The Church at the End.*

240. Brungs, *"Human Life."*

241. Ramsey, *Fabricating Man*, 1, 90ff, 122, 131; Gish, *Manipulating Life*, 28; Anderson, *Genetic Engineering*, 37.

242. Ramsey, *Fabricating Man*, 1, 90ff, 122, 131; Gish, *Manipulating Life.*

243. Ramsey, *"The Issues Facing Mankind,"* 42.

244. Payne, *Biblical/Medical Ethics*, 44-5.

245. *Ibid.*, 33-49.

246. *Ibid.*, 86.

247. *Ibid.*, 79-81.

248. *Ibid.*, 33-49.

249. Non-identical (fraternal) twins result from the fertilization of two eggs with two sperm. Obviously, the chromosomes of each pair are going to be considerably different.

250. Gish, *Manipulating Life*, 155-188.

251. Jones, *Brave New People*, 100-101; Ramsey, *Fabricating Man*, 68-72; Anderson, *Genetic Engineering*, 101-114.

252. Gish, *Manipulating Life*, 59-60.

253. Vaillant, *Adaptation to Life.*

254. Payne, *Biblical/Medical Ethics*, 144-152.

255. Randolph, *God Is Pro Life.*

256. *Ibid.*, 16-17.

257. Custance, "*The Widening Circle*," 126-129.

258. Morris, *The Biblical Basis*, 385-387.

259. Berkhof, *Systematic Theology*, 169-171.

260. Dillon, *The Inconstant Gene*, v-vi, 433-446.

261. Custance, "*Dauermodifications in Man,*" 219-249.

262. Clark, *Logic*, 1-6.

263. Morris, *The Biblical Basis of Modern Science*, 221-231 and Morris, *Studies in the Bible and Science*, 45-57.

264. Payne, *Biblical/Medical Ethics*, 76-79.

265. Gish, *Manipulating Life*, 173.

266. He conveyed this belief to me in a private conversation, but he may have said it in print in one of his many books.

267. Wilder-Smith, *The Natural Sciences.*

268. Morris, *The Biblical Basis of Modern Science*, 90.

269. Verbrugge, *Alive: An Enquiry*, 81-102. Verbrugge explains Herman Dooyeweerd's theory of "functors." These entities are systems (such as cells) that function according to their own "idionomy" or laws that are unique to their system. The only explanation for these functors is that God created them to function as they do. When the system is broken (for example, a cell membrane is punctured), the functor ceases to exist and becomes subject to the random laws of non-living matter.

270. Clark, *The Biblical Doctrine of Man*, 45.

271. Randolph, "*God Is Pro Life,*" 16-17.

272. The definition of regeneration includes sanctification and glorification as a continuation of the same spiritual process.

273. Payne, *Biblical/Medical Ethics*, p. 182-3.

274. Rushdoony, Rousas J., *Revolt Against Maturity*, Fairfax, VA: Thoburn Press, 1977, p. 110.

275. I am aware of the debates whether Christianity is a religion. I believe along with Gordon Clark that no category can be properly labelled "religion." Simply, religion is any personal philosophy held consciously or unconsciously. In our day certain words that are not preferable must be used in order to communicate. "Religion" is still useful for that purpose. The modern debate about the place of "religion" in society and politics, however, urgently mandates clarification of the definition.

276. Van Til, Cornelius, *Christian Theistic Ethics*, Phillipsburg: Presbyterian and Reformed Publishing Company, 1980, pp. 13-17.

277. Payne, *Biblical/Medical Ethics*, pp. 11-26.

278. North, Gary, *Unholy Spirits*, Ft. Worth, TX: Dominion Press, 1986.

279. The other causes of famine are: the prevention of cultivation or the willful destruction of crops, defective agriculture caused by communistic control of land, governmental interference by regulation or taxation, and currency restrictions, including debasing of the coin (inflation).

280. Payne, *Biblical/Medical Ethics*, pp. 90-94.

281. Bright, Bill, *"Jesus and the Intellectual"*, Campus Crusade for Christ, Inc., Arrowhead Springs, San Bernadino, CA 92404.

282. Grant, George, *Bringing in the Sheaves*, Atlanta, GA: American Vision Press, 1985.

283. "Sexually transmitted diseases" has replaced the term "venereal diseases," probably in an attempt to avoid the stigma of the latter.

284. Lynch, James L., *The Broken Heart*, New York: Basic Books, Inc., 1979

285. I am not arguing here for or against the death penalty in modern times for these offenses.

286. The complexities of what euthanasia is and is not is far beyond this book. I am using the term here as it would be used commonly: death brought on by an immediate act in a patient who otherwise would live for a time longer.

287. Adams, *Competent to Counsel*, pp. 141.

288. Stover, Eric and Elena O. Nightingale, *The Breaking of Bodies and Minds*, New York: W. H. Freeman and Company, 1985.

289. I am assuming the validity of "just wars" and capital punishment here. Obviously, these options will not exist for those Christians who hold other views. Most Christians will likely agree that killing in self-defense is right.

290. This emphasis on punishment suggests the reason that some studies have apparently demonstrated that the death penalty is not a deterrent to murder and other crimes. God did not intend it to be a deterrent, but a punishment to illustrate the value of life.

291. This re-orientation fundamentally concerns truth. Further, the basis of all ethics is some system of truth. However, a consideration of the relationship of truth and ethics here would cloud the issue under discussion.

292. A supplementary and more thorough list of these conclusions has already been developed. Payne, *Biblical/Medical Ethics*, pp. 95-96.

293. *The Larger and Shorter Catechisms of the Westminster Confession of Faith* are clear examples of the breadth of the application of the Ten Commandments. The reader who is not familiar with these catechisms should read them. He will be enriched and blessed by their content. I have briefly discussed this broader use of the Commandments elsewhere. Payne, *Biblical/Medical Ethics*, pp. 67-68.

BIBLIOGRAPHY

Chapter 1

Aristotle. *Politics* 1335b, trans. Ernest Barker (London: Oxford University Press, 1946), p. 327. Quoted by Richard Sherlock in "The Demographic Argument for Liberal Abortion Policies: Analysis of a Pseudo-Issue . . ."

Brackett, James and Harald Fredericksen. "Effects of Legalizing Abortion." *Lancet* 2:167-8, 1968.

Carlson, Allan C. "Famine 1985: 'Overpopulation' or Human Folly?" *The Presbyterian Journal* 43 (March 27): 6-7, 1985.

Carlson, Allan C. "The Malthusian Budget Deficit." *The Human Life Review* 11(3):35-47, 1985.

Chilton, David and Yonas Deressa. "Planned Famine in Ethiopia". *Biblical Economics Today* 8(3):1-4, 1985.

Clark, Colin. *Population and Land Use.* New York: St. Martin's, 1977.

Dillow, Joseph C. *Solomon on Sex.* Nashville: Thomas Nelson, 1981.

Eastland, Terry. "Who Put the Wrong in Wrongful Births." *The Human Life Review* 9(3): 69-80, 1983.

Finkelstein, Ed. "Hard Work Said to be Unpopular in 'Third World,'" *Tucson* (Arizona) *Herald*, November 25, 1971.

Grisez, Germain and Joseph M. Boyle, Jr. "Life, Death and Liberty." *The Human Life Review* 4(4):46-70, 1978.

Hilgers, Thomas W. and Dennis O'Hare. "Abortion Related Maternal Mortality: An In-Depth Analysis . . ."

Hook, Ernest B., Phillip K. Cross, and Dina M. Schreinemachers. "Chromosomal Abnormality Rates at Amniocentesis and in Live-Born Infants." *The Journal of the American Medical Association* 249 (April 15): 2034-2038, 1983.

Kazun, J. "The Population Bomb Threat: A Look at the Facts." *Intellect* 105 (June 1977): 412-414.

Kinsey, Alfred C., Wardell B. Pomeroy, et al. *Sexual Behavior in the Human Female.* Philadelphia: W. B. Saunders Co., 1953.

Kuehnelt-Leddihn, Erik von. "Some Reflections on Population Problems." *The Human Life Review* 3(1):71-84, 1977.

Marshall, Bob. *Playing God: Planned Parenthood and the Manipulation of Life and Death.* Westchester, Illinois: Good News Publications, 1987.

Levin, Robert J. and Amy Levin. "Sexual Pleasure: The Surprising Preferences of 100,000 Women." *Redbook Magazine* September 1975, 51-58.

Montgomery, John W.   "How to Decide the Birth-Control Question," *Christianity Today*, March 4, 1966, p. 10. Quoted in BCC, p. 23.

Muggeridge, Malcolm.   "The Overpopulation Myth." *The Human Life Review* 9(2): 116-119, 1983.

Norman, Colin. "Will World Population Double?" *Nature* 264 (November 4): 7-8, 1976.

Packer, J.I.   "Situations and Principles" In Bruce Kaye and Gordon Wenham, *Law, Morality and the Bible*, Downers Grove, Illinois: InterVarsity, 1978.

Potter, R.G. "Additional Births Averted When Abortion Is Added to Contraception". *Studies in Family Planning* 3(4):53-58, 1972.

Simon, Julian. "The Rhetoric of Population Control: Does the End Justify the Means?" *The Human Life Review* 9(4): 61-85, 1983.

Simon, Julian. *The Ultimate Resource*. Princeton University Press, 1981.

Smith, Janet E.   "Abortion as a Feminist Concern." *The Human Life Review* 4(3):62-76, 1978.

Smith, Robert D.   Book Review: *The Act of Marriage* by Tim and Beverly LaHaye. *The Journal of Pastoral Practice* 5(2): 43-49.

Tierney, John. "Fanisi's Choice." *Science 86* 7(1): 26-42, 1986.

Unger, Merrill F. and William White, Jr. "To Multiply, Increase". *Nelson's Expository Dictionary of the Old Testament*. Nashville: Thomas Nelson Publishers, 1980.

Wilson, Ellen. "Mother Didn't Know. *The Human Life Review* 4(4):25-33, 1978.

Young, R.V. "Literature, Literacy and Morality." *The Human Life Review* 9(1):46-66, 1983.

Chapter 2

Allen, David F. and Victoria Allen. *Ethical Issues in Mental Retardation*. Nashville: Abingdon, 1979.

Brackett, James and Harald Fredericksen. *"Effects of Legalizing Abortion."* Lancet 2:167-8, 1968.

Campolo, Anthony, Jr. *The Power Delusion*. Wheaton, IL: Victor Books, 1983.

Caravan, Francis. "History Repeats Itself." *The Human Life Review* 5(2):73-82, 1979.

Epps, Garrett. "Apostle of Abortion." *Science 82* (March):71-78, 1982.

Goldheizer, Joseph W., Armando de la Pena, C. Brandon Chenault, T. B. Woutersz. "Comparative Studies of the Ethynyl Estrogens Used in Oral Contraceptives II. Antiovulatory Potency." *American Journal of Obstetrics and Gynecology* 122: 619-624, 1975.

Grisez, Germain and Joseph M. Boyle, Jr. "Life, Death and Liberty." *The Human Life Review* 4(4):46-70, 1978.

Hatcher, Robert A., Gary K. Stewart, and Felicia Stewart. *Contraceptive Technology 1982-1983.* 11th Revised Edition. New York: Irvington Publishers, Inc., 1982.

Hilgers, Thomas W. and Dennis O'Hare. "Abortion Related Maternal Mortality: An In-Depth Analysis." *New Perspectives on Human Abortion.* Thomas W. Hilgers, Dennis J. Horan and David Mall. Frederick, MD: University Publications of America, 1981.

Marshall, Robert G. "Birth, Birth Control and Maternal Mortality." *All About Issues* 7(9):46-48, 1985. American Life League, P.O. Box 1350, Stafford, VA 22554.

Mosher, Steven Mosher. "Forced Abortions and Infanticide in Communist China." *The Human Life Review* 11(3)7-34, 1985.

Murad, Ferid and Robert C. Haynes, Jr. "Estrogens and Progestins." Alfred Goodman Gilman, Louis S. Goodman and Alfred Gilman, *The Pharmacological Basis of Therapeutics.* New York: Macmillan Publishing Co., pp. 1420-1447.

Murphy, William D., Emily M. Coleman, and Gene G. Abel. "Human Sexuality in the Mentally Retarded." In *Treatment Issues and Innovations in Mental Retardation.* New York: Plenum Press, 1983.

Ory, Howard W. "The Noncontraceptive Health Benefits from Oral Contraceptive Use." *Family Planning Perspecives* 14(4): 182-184.

Potts, Malcolm and Peter Diggory. *Textbook of Contraceptive Practice.* Cambridge: Cambridge University Press, 1983.

Ramsey, Paul. *Fabricated Man: The Ethics of Genetic Control.* New Haven, CN: Yale University Press, 1970.

Reed, Elizabeth W. and Sheldon C. Reed. *Mental Retardation: A Family Study.* Philadelphia: W. B. Saunders Company, 1965.

Robertson, John A. "Procreative Liberty and the Control of Conception, Pregnancy, and Childbirth." *Virginia Law Review* 69(3):405-434, 1983.

Sherlock, Richard. "The Demographic Argument for Liberal Abortion Policies: Analysis of a Pseudo-Issue." In *Hilgers*, pp. 450-465.

Simon, Julian. "The Rhetoric of Population Control: Does the End Justify the Means?" *The Human Life Review* 9(4): 61-85, 1983.

Smith, Janet E. "Abortion as a Feminist Concern." *The Human Life Review* 4(3):62-76, 1978.

Symposium, *Ethics and Medicine*. 1(1):4-14, 1985.

Uricchio, William A. *Natural Family Planning*. Washington: The Human Life Foundation, 1973.

Waltke, Bruce K. "Old Testament Texts Bearing on the Problem of the Control of Human Reproduction". Walter O. Spitzer and Carlyle L. Saylor. *Birth Control and the Christian: A Protestant Symposium on The Control of Human Reproduction*. Wheaton, IL: Tyndale House Publishers, 1969.

Chapter 3

Adams, Jay E. *Matters of Concern to Christian Counselors*. Phillipsburg, NJ: Presbyterian and Reformed Publishing Company, 1978, 3-4.

Anderson, J. Kerby. *Genetic Engineering*. Grand Rapids: Zondervan Publishing House, 1982.

Anderson, Norman. *Issues of Life and Death*. Downers Grove, IL: InterVarsity Press, 1974.

Anderson, Bruce L. *The Price of a Perfect Baby*. 2nd Edition. 1980. Minneapolis: Bethany House Publishers, 1984.

Collins, John A., William Wrixon, Lynn B. Janes, et al. "Treatment-Independent Pregnancy among Infertile Couples." *The New England Journal of Medicine* (November 17) 309: 1201-1206, 1983.

Curie-Cohen, Martin, Lesleigh Luttrell and Sander Shapiro. "Current Practice of Artificial Insemination by Donor in the United States." *The New England Journal of Medicine* (March 15) 300: 585-590, 1979.

Davis, John Jefferson. *Evangelical Ethics: Issues Facing the Church Today*. Phillipsburg, NJ: Presbyterian and Reformed Publishing Company, 1985.

Dunn, H. P. "Semen Examination." *Linacre Quarterly*, February 1987, 88-91.

"Father's Identity: The Right to Know." *Parade Magazine* July 29, 1984.

Fletcher, John C. "Artificial Insemination in Lesbians." *Archives of Internal Medicine* (March) 145:419-420, 1985.

"Insemination Policy Includes Singles." *American Medical News* October 10, 1980, 8.

Kaiser, Walter C. *Toward Old Testament Ethics*. Grand Rapids: Zondervan Publishing House, 1983.

Kristoff, Nicholas D. "Parents of 'Nobel Sperm' Baby." *The Washington Post* July 14, 1982, A-6. "The Sperm-Bank Scandal." *Newsweek* July 26, 1982, 4.

Mascola, Laurene and Mary E. Guinan. "Screening to Reduce Transmission of Sexually Transmitted Diseases in Semen Used for Artificial Insemination." *The New England Journal of Medicine* May 22, 314: 1354-1359, 1986.

Payne, Jr., Franklin E. *Biblical/Medical Ethics*. Milford, MI: Mott Media, 1985.

Polansky, Francis F., et al. "Do the Results of Semen Analysis Predict Future Fertility?" *Fertility and Sterility* 49:1059-1065, 1988.

Postma, E.G. *The Banner*, February 11, 1977 . Quoted in Regenmorter, *Dear God, Why Can't We Have a Baby*, 117.

Regenmorter, John and Sylvia, and Joe S. McIlhaney, Jr. *Dear God, Why Can't We Have a Baby?* Grand Rapids: Baker Book House, 1986.

Thielicke, Helmut. *Theological Ethics: Politics*. Vol. 2. Ed. William H. Lazareth. Grand Rapids: William B. Eerdmans Publishing Company, 1969.

Wallis, C. and O. Friedrich. "The New Origins of Life." *Time* September 10, 1984, 46-56.

Yussman, Marvin A. "Principles and Procedures of Artificial Insemination." *Contemporary* OB/GYN 5(3): 107-117, 1975.

Chapter 4

Anderson, K. "Genetic Genesis: Test-tube Babies." Probe Ministries International, 1979.

Berry, J. E. Testimony before the Ethics Advisory Board. *Human Life Review* 5 (4) 1979:97.

"British Physicians Criticize Test-tube Baby Pioneer." *American Medical News* (October 8, 1982):18.

Bronson, R. A. "Current Limitations of In Vitro Fertilization." *Resident and Staff Physician* 30 (5):(May 1984):19-23.

Brungs, R. A. "Biotechnology and the Social Order." *Human Life Review* 5 (1) 1979:31-50.

Ethics Committeee of the American Fertility Society. "Ethical Considerations of the New Reproductive Technologies." *Fertility and Sterility* (September) 46(3), Supplement 1, 1986.

Gantt, P. A., J. A. Hill, and P. G. McDonough. "Reversal of Female Sterilization." *Southern Medical Journal* 75 (February 1982):161-163.

Gold, M. "The Baby Makers." *Science 85* 6 (April 1985):26-38.

Harlow, H. F. "Ethology." In *Comprehensive Textbook of Psychiatry*, edited by H. I. Kaplan, A. M. Freedman, and B. J. Sadock, 424-443. Baltimore: Williams and Wilkins, 1980.

Hodgen, G. D. "In Vitro Fertilization." *Journal of the American Medical Association* 246 (August 7, 1981):590-597.

Marrs, R. P. "In Vitro Fertilization-Embryo Replacement." Paper presented at the Annual Clinical Meeting of the American College of Obstetricians and Gynecologists, Washington, D.C., May 11-12, 1985.

Nelson, R. M. "The Ethics of In Vitro Fertilization and Embryo Transfer." *Christian Medical Society Journal* 14 (1) 1983:19-25, 32.

Ramsey, Paul. "On In Vitro Fertilization." *Human Life Review* 5 (1) 1979:17-30.

Rushdoony R. J. *Salvation and Godly Rule*. Vallecito, CA: Ross House Books, 1984.

Rust, M. "Fertility Treatment Advances Stir Ethical Decisions." *American Medical News* (November 16, 1984):3, 29-30.

Schlesselman, J. J. "How Does One Assess the Risk of Abnormalities from Human In Vitro Fertilization?" *American Journal of Obstetrics and Gynecology* 135 (September 1979):135-148.

Shaw, J. "Handling of Embryos Generates Ethics Debate." *American Medical News* (May 27, 1983): 1, 7-8.

Steinfels, M. O. "In Vitro Fertilization: 'Ethically Acceptable' Research." *Hastings Center Report* (June) 9: 7, 1979.

Studdard, A. "The Morality of In Vitro Fertilization." *Human Life Review* 5 (4) 1979:41-55.

Thielicke, Helmut. *Theological Ethics: Politics*. Vol. 2. Ed. William H. Lazareth. Grand Rapids: William B. Eerdmans Publishing Company, 1969.

Tiefel, H. O. "Human In Vitro Fertilization: A Conservative View." *Journal of the American Medical Association* 247 (June 18, 1982):3235-3242.

Timnick, L. "Surrogate Money, Atonement." *Los Angeles Times*, June 7, 1981. Quoted in Anderson, *The Price of a Perfect Baby*, p. 31.

Utian, Wulf H., Leon Sheean, James M. Goldfarb, *et al.* "Successful Pregnancy after In Vitro Fertilization and Embryo Transfer from an Infertile Woman to a Surrogate." *The New England Journal of Medicine* (November 21) 313: 1351-1352, 1985.

Wallis, C. and O. Friedrich. "The New Origins of Life." *Time* (September 10, 1984):46-56.

Walters, LeRoy. "Editor's Introduction." *The Journal of Medicine and Philosophy* 10: 209-212, 1985.

Wilson, E. "Seeing Through the Glass." *Human Life Review* 5 (4) 1979: 56-65.

Chapters 5 - 7

Anderson, W. French. "Human Gene Therapy: Scientific and Ethical Considerations." *The Journal of Medicine and Philosophy* 10:275-291, 1985.

Anderson, J. Kerby. *Genetic Engineering*. Grand Rapids: Zondervan Publishing House, 1982.

Anderson, W. French. "Prospects for Human Gene Therapy". *Science* 226:401-409, 1984.

Atkinson, David "Some Theological Perspectives on the Human Embryo (Part I)". *Ethics and Medicine* 2:8-10, 1986.

Berkhof, L., *Systematic Theology*, Grand Rapids: Wm. B. Eerdmans Publishing Co., 1939. pp. 202-10.

Brungs, Robert. "Human Life vs. Human Personhood." *The Human Life Review* 8(3):70-80, 1982.

Calvin, John, *Institutes of the Christian Religion*. Vol. I. Trans. by Henry Beveridge, Grand Rapids: Eerdmans Publishing Company, 1979, pp. 162-167.

Chinnici, Madeline. "The Promise of Gene Therapy." *Science Digest*. May
    1985, pp. 48-51, 88-9.
Clark, Gordon H., *The Biblical Doctrine of Man*, Jefferson, MD: The
    Trinity Foundation, 1984, pp. 5-19.
Clark, Gordon H., *Logic*. Jefferson, MD: The Trinity Foundation, 1985.
Copi, Irving M., *Introduction to Logic*.   6th Ed. 1953.   New York:
    MacMillan Publishing Co., Inc., 1982.
Custance, Arthur C. "Who Taught Adam to Speak." *Genesis and Early
    Man*. Grand Rapids, MI: Zondervan Publishing Company, 1975, 250-
    271.
Dillon, Lawrence S. *The Genetic Mechanism and the Origin of Life*. New
    York: Plenum Press, 1978.
Dillon, Lawrence S. *Ultrastructure, Macromolecules, and Evolution*. New
    York: Plenum Press, 1981.
Dillon, Lawrence S. *The Inconstant Gene*. New York: Plenum Press,
    1983.
Fletcher, John C. "Ethical Issues in and Beyond Prospective Clinical Trials
    of Human Gene Therapy." *The Journal of Medicine and Philosophy*
    10:293-309, 1985.
Friedrick, Otto. "What Do Babies Know?" *Time* (August 15, 1983) pp. 52-
    59.
Gish, Duane T. and Clifford Wilson. *Manipulating Life: Where Does It
    Stop*. San Diego: Master Books, 1981.
Grobstein, Clifford. "The Early Development of Human Embryos." *The
    Journal of Medicine and Philosophy* 10-213-236, 1985.
Iglesias, Teresa. "What Kind of Being is the Human Embryo?" *Ethics and
    Medicine* 2(1):2-7, 1986.
Jones, D. Gareth. *Brave New People*. Downers Grove, IL: InterVarsity
    Press, 1984.
Judson, Horace Freeland. "Who Shall Play God?" *Science Digest*, May
    1985, pp. 52, 55, 83, 91.
Kelly, Thadeus E. *Clinical Genetics and Genetic Counseling*.   2nd Ed.,
    Chicago: Year Book Medical Publishers, Inc., 1986.

Kuyper, Abraham, *The Work of the Holy Spirit*. Trans. by J. Hendri De Vries, Reprint. Funk and Wagnalls Company, 1900. Grand Rapids: Eerdmans Publishing Company, 1979, pp. 203-251.

Mertz, Beverly. "Stumbling Blocks Pave Path to Clinical Trials for Gene Therapy." *The Journal of the American Medical Association* 255: 1825-32.

Morris, Henry M. *Studies in the Bible and Science*. Phillipsburg, PA: Presbyterian and Reformed Publishing Company, 1966.

Murray, John, *Collected Writings*. Vol II., Edinburgh: The Banner of Truth Trust, 1976, pp. 34-46.

National Institutes of Health. "Recombinant DNA Molecules Research, Proposed Actions Under Guidelines: Notice." August 19, 1985. Federal Register, pp. 33462-7.

President's Commission for the Study of Ethical Problems in Medicine and Biomedical and Behavorial Research. "Screening and Counseling for Genetic Conditions: The Ethical, Social, and Legal Implications of Genetic Screening, Counseling, and Educational Programs. Washington, DC: Superintendent of Documents. U. S. Government Printing Office, 20402.

Ramsey, Paul. "The Issues Facing Mankind." *Ethics and Medicine: A Christian Perspective* 1(3):37-43, 1985.

Ramsey, Paul. *Fabricated Man: The Ethics of Genetic Control*. New Haven, CT: Yale University Press, 1970.

Randolph, William. "God is Pro Life". *The Journal of Pastoral Practice* 3(3):9-27, 1979.

Schaeffer, Francis. *The Church at the End of the 20th Century*. 2nd Edition., Downers Grove, IL: InterVarsity Press, 1985.

Sky Magazine. "The Marvelous Chip". *Sky*, May 1984, p. 38.

Sobran, Joseph. "Eugenics and Euphemisms." *The Human Life Review* 8(3):117-118, 1982.

Stambrook, Peter J. "What the Clinician Needs to Know about DNA." Presentation at "Clinical Genetics for Practitioners," at Kiawah Island, July 27, 1984.

Taur, Carol A. "Personhood and Human Embryos and Fetuses." *The Journal of Medicine and Philosophy* 10:253-266, 1985.

Valliant, George E. *Adaptation to Life*. Boston: Little, Brown and Company, 1977.

Verbrugge, Magnus. *Alive: An Enquiry into the Origin and Meaning of Life*. Vallectito, CA: Ross House Books, 1984.

Wilder-Smith, A. E. *The Natural Sciences Know Nothing of Evolution*. San Diego: Master Books, 1981.

Wilder-Smith, A. E. "Origin of the Genetic Code." (Lecture tape). San Diego: Master Books, 1983.

Watson, James D., John Tooze and David T. Kurtz. *Recombinant DNA: A Short Course*. New York: Scientific American Books, 1983.